Revelations on the River

Revelations on the River

Healing a Nation, Healing Ourselves

Matthew Dowd

Skyhorse Publishing

Skyhorse Publishing books may be purchased in bulk at special discounts for sales promotion, corporate gifts, fund-raising, or educational purposes. Special editions can also be created to specifications. For details, contact the Special Sales Department, Skyhorse Publishing, 307 West 36th Street, 11th Floor, New York, NY 10018 or info@skyhorsepublishing.com.

Skyhorse® and Skyhorse Publishing® are registered trademarks of Skyhorse Publishing, Inc.®, a Delaware corporation.

Visit our website at www.skyhorsepublishing.com.

10 9 8 7 6 5 4 3 2 1

Library of Congress Cataloging-in-Publication Data is available on file.

Cover design by Kai Texel

Print ISBN: 978-1-5107-6863-5
Ebook ISBN: 978-1-5107-6864-2

Printed in the United States of America

Contents

Contents

Introduction

rev·e·la·tion
/ˌrevəˈlāSH(ə)n/

noun

*"a surprising and previously unknown fact, especially one that is made known
in a dramatic way."*
*"the divine or supernatural disclosure to humans of something relating to
human existence or the world."*

As I sit in my home on a few secluded acres nestled on the
Blanco River here in Central Texas, amidst the Cypress, Live
Oak and Pecan trees, I contemplate the slogan of the small
rural town where I live—"a little piece of heaven"—and what
it means to hear the voice of the divine and the truths I have
uncovered walking on the earth beneath the heavens above.

Revelation is a concept that has unfortunately become
captive to certain followers of religious faiths. Far too many
adherents of religion use their "sacred words" taken from texts
written hundreds or thousands of years ago as the end all and

be all of revelation and only accept their view of the divine word of God as truth. In truth it is a word that applies moment to moment as each of us journeys through life in this mystery of our universe. Revelation doesn't only have to be about the Apocalypse of John or the Book of Revelation, likely written in the first century AD. It is important that we consider both of the dictionary definitions of revelation listed above, and consequently a much more open concept of divine intervention or of any revelation than just what we presuppose from religion.

Further, we can accept the idea of an epiphany that doesn't solely have to do with the Epiphany in religious circles of the manifestation of Christ to the gentiles through the three Wise Men. Our epiphanies can be religious in nature, but often they are much more secular. For those of you not religious you are already much more open to insights that aren't convinced by the divine, and for those of us who practice a faith let's temporarily suspend the religious roots of epiphany and look at it through the broader definition of "a usually sudden manifestation or perception of the essential nature or meaning of something, an intuitive grasp of reality through something (such as an event) usually simple and striking, or an illuminating discovery, realization, or disclosure."

I am a person immersed in a faith tradition, whose faith has been dear and consequential to me throughout my life, with an additional link of having been an altar boy and altar server through my youth growing up in Michigan. I still attend weekly service on Sundays (with the divine exception granted during Covid), and I believe in the concept of divine revelation. However, logic and intuition inform me that if I believe in an omnipotent and omniscient force in the universe, I must not limit my conception of where insights can be garnered by my own structures or boxes.

Why would one accept only revelation or epiphany that came a few thousand years ago in the form of an inspired Bible (Old and New Testaments) to one tribe, at one time, and in one way? Wouldn't God (or whatever name you give the divine) want to reveal truths at many times in divergent ways and faith traditions? Isn't the act of creation revelation in itself, and the beauty of our world a constant form of epiphany?

My own faith opens me up to understanding that God is constantly attempting to communicate with us about the truth of the universe. God is doing this through all faiths as well as through the presence of compassionate and kind people in this world, and even through those who are not kind but are gifts nonetheless. Sometimes we pick up on the messages and let them settle into our hearts and souls. Some of us may even write them down so that generations that follow might benefit from our revelations.

I have tapped into much of the divine revelation as I have read and studied the Bible of my own faith of Catholicism and Christianity, but I have also seen revelation in the Gilluy Shekinah of Judaism, the Bhagavad Gita of Hinduism, the teachings of the Buddha, the Koran of our Islamic sisters and brothers, the wisdom of the Native Americans, and in so many various faith traditions. For me, there are a thousand paths to get to the mountain top, and none is more right than another. Some paths may be smooth, but take you longer. Other paths may be shorter, but have steep inclines. Still others may take you into a grove of trees, while some may bring you by a stream or mountain lake. Each path has its own beauty, struggle and truth. All lead to the same destination at the summit of peace.

And there is also revelation of the truth of the universe from scientists, artists, writers or poets who may have no religion but reveal aspects of the universe we did not understand before. And revelation or epiphany can come to us in significant ways in our day to day walk through life as we encounter others on the trails and travails of our short human existence. Revelations can also be made known to us in a deep way even as we sit by the natural beauty of a lake, speaking to us in a sunrise or sunset in the words of the waves, or on a hillside or mountain top as we feel the earth beneath our feet.

Revelation to me isn't limited by the timing of the divine or by some other force in the universe we are presently unaware of; it is only limited if we lack openness to the world and within ourselves. It is limited by how closed off we are to listening to the voices sometimes very quietly trying to convey some aspect of life or a truth of the universe. When we only accept revelation in certain forms at certain times, and shut down our minds, hearts and souls because we think we have all the answers already, we will easily miss out on a better understanding of this world and of life in general.

I have often in life operated from a place of an over-reliance on certainty, whether that was in my personal life or in my political life, and in my speaking and writing. In politics, I have encountered many on both sides of the aisle who hold tightly to dogma or ideology. They allow these ideologies to get in the way of a more thorough understanding of the present moment and what might be needed to achieve progress. It is these dogmas or ideology that cause much of the division and bitterness that are far too widespread in our country today. Having all the answers based in a dogma not only prevents us from opening up to new answers or epiphanies that may better fit the world, it doesn't even let us ask the right questions or know that there are still questions to be asked.

I have come to understand that the opposite of faith isn't doubt—the opposite of faith is certainty. Revelations are not about unveiling or discovering certainties, but in illuminating in new ways what we might have missed or overlooked before. It is about an epiphany that causes us to reconsider or look with new eyes. Throughout history, the people of greatest faith also harbored many doubts. Whether it be a person of religion or a secular person in search of knowledge, it is the doubts that drove them to greater understanding as well as the acceptance of the mystery of life. It wasn't certainty that caused them to keep wandering and searching for truth; it was the knowing that they didn't know, and weren't always sure.

I find many of those who are religious and seem to have all the answers don't operate from a place of doubt, but from a place of absolute certainty. If you are certain about the existence of God or the stories conveyed in sacred books, why do you need faith? Certainty gets in the way of greater connection to the divine or to wisdom, and it blocks us from deeper connection with others who may not believe exactly as we do.

Mother Teresa, deemed a saint by the Catholic Church, was a person of great faith, self-sacrifice, service and virtue, and she had many doubts throughout her life. This is revealed so clearly in her personal letters published after her death. Martin Luther King, Jr., a minister and civil rights icon, was a man of immense faith and conviction, and also carried many doubts and conflicts about faith with him. Gandhi led throughout his life with deep faith, and was not afraid to experience and express doubt.

When we look around and consider how we are going to live our own lives and lead in a compassionate way, we find the most effective leaders who initiated profound change in the world to be those who had a faith in something bigger than themselves, and carried and examined many doubts in their hearts and minds. These leaders, as each of us can be, were open to learning more, growing in their lives and leadership, and being receptive to any revelations that might come.

So, with a great sense of humility, I would like to lay out some things I have come to know through my own revelations as I have lived these many years in my flawed humanity. I have learned them through the trials and tribulations, the pleasures and pains of life, and in staying still long enough to really listen. In walks on the river near me now, in strolls through the woods, in connection with others, in time on the Great Lakes surrounding Michigan, and even in smoking a cigar in the quiet sitting in a rocker on my porch...something moved me in these moments to dive inward and seek understanding.

For many people who encounter me in life, they have put me in a convenient box of political strategist or commentator. Or they know I have been married and divorced twice, or that I grew up in a rather dysfunctional family of 11 children, or that I lost two children in tragic circumstances, and that the twin daughter who survived started life with nine months in a neonatal unit. Some people know me by the good I have done, and others know me by the mistakes I have made. Yes, those are all aspects of who I was, or, in part, of who I am today, but like each of you, there is much more to ourselves than a label or a profession or personal circumstance that defines us in the years of our existence.

For myself, and I hope you as well, I try to let go of the labels I have used in my past or that were used to describe me. Some days I pursue the heart of a poet within me, and other days I like to see myself as having the soul of a prophet, while some days I feel the pagan roots of my Celtic ancestry. I don't compare myself to leaders in the past who have been poets or prophets, but for us leading in the present, we each can listen to the song within us that calls us to truth, and we can embrace roles that we don't often share with the world.

I have discovered many of these revelations or epiphanies in the darkness of night and life, and many in the sunrise and sunset of days when light came into my heart. I have had some of these revelations in a profound connection with a fellow human being, in walking through the beauty of nature, in the day-to-day observations with my children, and sometimes sitting quietly in a church or another sacred place, or sitting under the stars listening to the musings on science and space.

The ten topic areas I have chosen to explore in the pages of this book can only be explained by the fact each of them became clearer through many great loves and losses on this trail of time of my brief existence on this planet we all call home. The hymn "Amazing Grace" has always spoken to me in so many ways because it really is a path to revelation. "I was lost, and now I am found" captures well what we are going through in our struggles in life, and we become "found" when we arrive at a place of understanding and some truth in life is revealed to us. This understanding and truth puts in context all the disparate circumstances we have been through.

I also love "Amazing Grace" because the man who wrote it went through his own path of revelation and redemption. Jon

Newton, before he wrote down the hymn, was a slave boat captain who, for many years, profited off transporting African people in bondage in absolutely horrific ways to a place where they had no freedom and were subjected to such appalling abuse. Newton finally came to a point that his doubts and his guilt overwhelmed him, and some truths were revealed so that he could no longer keep doing what he was doing. This revelation set him on a path of righting his wrongs. I recommend reading more on the path of Newton because it is a complicated journey that doesn't often lend itself to a simple explanation.

In my last book, *A New Way: Embracing the Paradox as We Lead and Serve*, written in 2016 and released in the beginning of 2017, I started out with this in my introduction: "We are in a crucial moment. America is at a crossroads. And so is each of us. We are in a time of tremendous disruption, frustration, anxiety, and confusion. There is ongoing civil discord and divisiveness. We feel disconnected from our own hearts, from one another, and from the values that leaders have spoken and written about for thousands of years. Institutions—financial, economic, political, governmental—are crumbling around us.

We have simultaneously lost faith in nearly every institution that in the past bound us together and helped lead us. Many of us feel like orphans, in search of both community and a new brand of leadership. We know in our hearts that there has to be a leadership out there based in integrity, but we keep coming up empty."

Boy, did I underestimate the last four years since that was written, especially the year of 2020. I could not have imagined that we would have simultaneously faced a global pandemic, an economic meltdown with millions going unemployed and thousands and thousands of businesses shut down, and an insurrection at the United States Capitol where the chambers were taken over by an armed mob and people killed.

In the midst of this, schools were shut down, we couldn't gather in restaurants or in groups of any kind, churches were closed, grocery stores established entirely new protocols and set limits on purchases, and those of us who didn't lose jobs had to learn to work remotely. We couldn't travel for fun or work, we couldn't visit our relatives in nursing homes, and we couldn't even hug each other.

Anxieties, frustrations, sadness and anger rose in different waves and at different times for each of us. We struggled to cope and adapt in this wholesale disruption. For each of us, maybe for the first time, we started asking ourselves very intro-spective questions: Is my life centered in the right ways? Where can I find meaning? What is the truth of it all? Who should I listen to? Is it time to make changes in my life to seek a more meaningful existence? How do I structure my life going forward after all this? What really inspires me?

As we move forward in the months and years ahead with some renewed hope with the Coronavirus at this time more under control, beginning again to gather and hug and connect, and with new leadership in Washington bringing more calm and less chaos, I wanted to convey some of my revelations in these ten topic areas: love, trauma, past/present/future, ends/means, faith/science, light and dark, forgiveness, concentric circles, legacy, and interconnection.

Why these ten? In so many discussions I've had, we all seem to keep coming back to the universality of these subjects as well as how they inform how we might adjust our individual paths in this time of mixed feelings in an uncertain world.

The discussions and deliberations around these topics led me to make some changes in my own life. One big one I made was to leave ABC News, where I was Chief Political Analyst, in January 2021. This was a place I had called home for work for nearly 14 years. I had to adapt in 2020, in analysis of the elections, to more remote discussions from my hometown, and also watch how people were coping with all the change happening all around us and the assaults on our democracy and our constitutional principles.

In addition, though it wasn't the primary cause of my leaving ABC News, I have been the subject of many death threats because of my criticisms of the past administration. In fact, I received a call from the Federal Bureau of Investigation after they apprehended the infamous Florida pipe-bomber, Cesar Sayoc, who had targeted critics of President Trump. The FBI informed me I was on that targeted list found at his home, and they advised me not to open any packages for which I didn't know the sender. Further, on multiple occasions, the former President and key members of his staff attempted to get me fired from my job at ABC because of my criticisms and what I saw as truth telling. I decided, as I was working on a book exploring the truths of these ten elements of life, that job no longer fit me and neither did it coincide with the energy I wanted to expend toward a life of meaning.

The other change I made was much smaller and simpler. In every other year I would quickly take down my Christmas tree after Little Christmas or Epiphany on January 6, and return my home to the way it was before. The tree, with its white lights and the way it filled my space, brought me such warmth and joy every time I looked at it. So, I have removed the ornaments and left the tree up with its lights; it sits here behind my shoulder as I write these words. I decided I didn't care what others thought about having a Christmas tree up all year because it had meaning to me. The hundreds of lights on the tree also convey to me a symbolism of all the different ways the light of life can reveal truth or meaning to us, and that epiphany can be a daily encounter.

And with my daughter now finishing her senior year of high school after an unprecedented year of challenges, and about to step into the next chapter of her life as she goes to college, I thought it was a good time to reflect on these important values and determine their alignment with my life as it unfolds in the years ahead. My interactions with her through her now eighteen years have given me so many revelations and epiphanies on many of the ten topic areas we are about to delve into here.

We learn along the way not only from real people in our daily lives, or from stories from history or historical figures, but also from fiction and myths of today and long ago. As the fictional character Emily Thorne, in the television series *Revenge* said, "Revelations help us accept the things we need the most, expose the secrets we so desperately try to hide and illuminate the dangers all around us. But more than anything, revelations are windows into our true selves...of the good and the evil and those wavering somewhere in between."

I hope to convey my own understanding of some deeper wisdom in the universe. And in this conversation with you, maybe we can each discover some additional knowledge of the mysteries of ourselves and how we might better lead in our circles of life. Or maybe this conversation will open us up a little bit more to have empathy for and understanding of others. And help us identify the aspects of other leaders we might want to choose in politics, business, or in any organization we might be involved or engaged.

Maybe in your reading of my humble words and thoughts, it might cause you to pause and become open to your own revelations or epiphanies. Each of us can be a divining rod for the divine. It doesn't take a prophet over there somewhere or in a time gone by to tell us truths; we can become in many ways the prophets of our own path and intersect with the revelations that are occurring in each moment.

Welcome aboard, and let's do this....

Strewn About

A petrified rock
Arrowheads broken
Quartz in dirt
An old leather strap
A rusted license plate
From decades ago
Walking the land
Between a rise
And a river
A vacant birdhouse
Which has seen
Loftier days
Rusty nails
Broken glass
A hawk feather
Stuck in the green

What we find
Should we keep
Each revealing
Some truth unknown
At least for
This moment
I hold
…as dear.

1
Love

*"To **love** at all is to be vulnerable. **Love** anything and your heart will be wrung and possibly broken. If you want to make sure of keeping it intact you must give it to no one, not even an animal. Wrap it carefully round with hobbies and little luxuries; avoid all entanglements."*

The famed British writer C. S. Lewis, who was born in Belfast, Ireland, wrote these words in his popular book *The Four Loves*. This book analyzes love, from both a religious and philosophical perspective. Interestingly, though born an Anglican, Lewis became an atheist in his teen years; he then returned to Christianity later in life with a much deeper understanding of love, developed through his own heartbreak and journey.

What can I add to this topic that has been felt, discussed, celebrated, and pondered by not only the brilliance of C. S. Lewis, but countless others throughout the millennia of human existence?

Poets and authors before and after Lewis have written of love, spanning the romantic to the divine—William Butler Yeats, Emily Dickinson, Rumi, Mary Oliver, William Shakespeare,

Martin Luther King, Jr., Pablo Neruda, and thousands more. Love and seeking an understanding of love are part of nearly every sacred text passed down from generation to generation, from the teachings of loving God and each other to how love might be defined in practice.

Take some time to read the verses of the Quran and what the Prophet Muhammad related about love, or sit with the Song of Songs in the Bible or Jesus' words in the Gospels. Peruse the words of Hindu or Buddhist texts, study the lessons suggested by Confucius, or immerse yourself in the wisdom of Native Americans. All speak of love and its power in the universe.

Artists, whether in music or painting or sculpture, have created beauty in sound and form to explain to us concepts of love. Scientific thinkers and philosophers delve into love and seek to understand and explain its strength and power. Learned medical professionals, from researchers to physicians to nurses, see the healing power of love in healthcare settings, and attempt to gauge it with data. Children who have never read, studied, or discussed the nuances of love respond intuitively to the lessons of love as they are exposed to it at birth, or feel its scarcity when not present. When my children first grasped my hand as infants, and later as young children, the feeling of the exchange of love was undeniable.

We each have loved and lost, fallen into or out of love, found love that lasted a day, or a season, or a lifetime. We have loved and tried to explain the love of a parent, a sibling, a child, a partner, our vision of the Almighty, a landscape, a song, our work or mission, service to another...the list is endless.

We each have an innate desire to love and be loved that we travel through life with; even in those times we doubt how real and true love actually is in our own worlds, we still have some innate drive toward it. We sense its power when it overwhelms our hearts, and we sense its lack when it seems to disappear. Often, we move through the world measuring our existence purely based on experiencing either an abundance of love in our life or a paucity of it.

The stories of love's power and mankind's searching for it are probably what first began our conversations around a campfire outside of a cave as we struggled to survive a hundred thousand years ago as hunters and gatherers. I know today every time I am gathered around a campfire with folks, in some way the tales of love and loss are invariably what underlie every story.

I am a huge fan of the play and story of Camelot. Not the one referring to President John F. Kennedy's administration and powerful people around tables at the White House, but the mythical story from England of long ago, and all the tales told of the Knights of the Roundtable. This original *Camelot* is the tragic love story of Sir Lancelot and Queen Guinevere, which not only affected the individuals involved including King Arthur, but it also nearly brought down an entire kingdom with its entanglements.

The forces of love in this story, and really every story, took over with passion and purpose, and the participants were swept along in this powerful river of some unknown destiny. Even when their minds tried to navigate and adjust the path and its potential destruction of the stability in Camelot, they could not dispel the truth of authentic love. Just as the river outside my window sweeps down a valley carrying with it pieces of the land and banks, love swept up the people in this play, and it became a story told from generation to generation.

Through the tumult of 2021, we observed a love story of a father and a son and a country. It was not a tale about the prolonging of a monarchy but of preserving a democracy and defending our democratic institutions. Congressman Jamie Raskin, whose father was an aide in the modern Camelot of the President Kennedy administration, lost his son to suicide just as he was about to embark on being the lead of the Impeachment managers involved in the trial of President Donald Trump. And as he was on the verge of becoming a household name in the trial, he publicly took a moment to express, in such a sincere and compelling way, the love he had in the aftermath of his son Tommy's death. Representative Raskin's son left behind a note saying, "Please look after each other, the animals and the global poor for me. All my love, Tommy."

We know this Jewish constitutional lawyer Representative Raskin, who has been at times described as a humanist or an atheist, operates from a deep faith in something bigger than self and comes from a place of understanding of spiritual love. Raskin also demonstrates in his life of public service an inherent love of country and humanity. But Raskin was brought to his knees, broken open by the simple yet powerful love for his son, and maybe more importantly of his son's love for him. As he said in his closing argument in the trial, "Our reputations and our legacy will be inextricably intertwined with what we do here, and with how you exercise your oath to do impartial justice. I know and trust you will do impartial justice, driven by meticulous attention to the overwhelming facts of the case and your love of our Constitution, which I know dwells in your heart. 'The times have found us,' said Tom Paine, the namesake of my son. The times have found us. Is this America? What kind of America will this be? It's literally in our hands. God-speed to the Senate of the United States."

Let me start with my conception of the love relationship with God. Many of us have been taught that we must love God, and worship God, and then from that we will know we are loved. Leaders in faith communities and even in our own family upbringing frequently teach us that we owe it to God to love him or her or it. We are told that God is so amazing and awe inspiring that our love for God is demanded, and an expression of that love is required both in private and public settings. I actually think this standard faith expression of God and love reverses what we are ultimately called toward.

If God is omniscient and the be-all and end-all, the Alpha and Omega, the Beginning and the End, the Most High, the Supreme Divinity, the Pure, and the Perfection, then why would God care if some insignificant aspect of his or her creation loves upwards toward the heavens. If God is everything and can do anything, he or she really wouldn't care if we loved it, worshipped it, or prostrated ourselves before it. And why would God have a need to be worshipped if God is full unto itself?

One day when I was hiking in the Cascade mountains of Washington state and watching my younger sister's son play so joyfully, purely and innocently amidst the tall trees that fill the Pacific Northwest, it filled me with such incredible beauty and a feeling of God's love for each of us. A feeling very disconnected from my worship of God, or my need to offer love to God, but just an acceptance of what already was true.

My insight into this relationship with God is that in order for us to be fulfilled we must first know we are loved by God. That no matter where we are in life, our ups or downs, our flaws or our finest moments, we know we are loved. It is in that feeling or knowing we are loved that we are fundamentally transformed and experience peace of mind, especially in troubled times or challenging circumstances.

And if this type of knowing love—understanding and accepting we are loved—is the real call of God, then why wouldn't that apply in our human interactions with others. Maybe the greatest positive impact in a person comes not so much in loving but knowing and trusting they are loved. I have witnessed so many people in life who had a huge capacity to love, but were not able to know they were loved, to allow another's love to land in such a way that they were able to accept the deep truth of it. And for years I put myself in this category of trying to love but not trusting I was loved.

For me, love isn't a destination, but the actual path we are on. It is the strongest energy operating in the universe, the way the divine communicates across creation. It is somewhat like the "force" in Star Wars, which extends to all beings and matter, and it is for us to figure out how we tap into its power and flow with love as it fills everything known and unknown.

Too often in relationships, we think love is the goal, when in reality it is the way. I have redefined one of my own crucial goals to feel and embrace the unity of everything as one, with love as the way to get to that interconnectedness and shared reality. If someone breaks up with us, we often fall into the trap of believing that person must have never loved us. What happens if we believed that whenever someone loved us or we loved them, that no matter how that season of our life finished, that love was always and is always real?

Each of us has had our heart broken in some way in a love relationship. This heartbreak could be the loss of a child, parent or a sibling (I have experienced all three in my life), the abrupt end of a partnership, a betrayal in life of someone we trusted. Our hearts can break if we lose faith in someone we trusted in politics or an organization. The heart can be torn or broken when we see the destruction of natural beauty, or injustice or violence.

The question is not *if* we are going to have loves that end in heartbreak, or how we protect ourselves from inevitable loss in loving relationships, but what is our response to our hearts being broken?

If we are a person who believes in the power of love, in its clear reality, even when impermanent, then should we allow ourselves to become bitter and distrusting when our hearts break? Should we allow our hearts to grow smaller, and to stop believing in love? In the immediate aftermath of heartbreak, yes, we are incredibly sad and confused, often questioning what was real, and wondering how to move forward in life with love. That is natural and necessary.

And then the moment comes thereafter of a choice we have. Do we allow our heart to open and love again? Do we repair the breaks in our heart, and know that our heart will grow bigger and stronger in the aftermath of the breaks? Can we become more compassionate to others because of our own loss, and allow ourselves to love even deeper?

If we are broken by loss, then the love was real; otherwise, it would not have affected us in such a wrenching way. To understand love is to look at our own response, not at what someone else did. If I have given my authentic love to another, their response, although flawed or even motivated by selfish ends, doesn't change the reality of my own love and heart unless we allow another's darkness to diminish our own light. We prove love's ultimate truth, not just in the joy it brings, but in our response to heartbreak in life.

Many understand and experience love in vastly different ways, depending on whether they are loving an individual or many. I have seen many "leaders" in my journey who have an incredible capacity to love and care for 500 or 5,000 or five million souls, but who are lost when it comes to caring for just one soul in an intimate relationship. They break their back helping others in our country or communities, but when it comes to loving just one person close to them, they are ill-equipped or fearful of carrying that load.

For me, throughout much of my life, I have been very good at loving others or working for others as long as they didn't get too close or demand too much in an intimate way. I could help you, and I could love from a distance, but I stumbled when it came to loving and trusting up close. I believed in true love and had a dream of it, but didn't actually open myself to it or practice it.

So many of us going through life, and in the varied relationships we encounter, seem to have a very easy time giving a compliment, but an incredibly difficult time receiving one. In a very similar way, we might love and then be unwilling to accept the love of another human being. A sure sign of our unwillingness to accept the love given by God or by another or even through the beauty in nature is how comfortable we are when someone compliments us. Or in how quickly we return the compliment, leaving no space between the love given and our need to give love back.

It took heartbreak in my life along the path I was walking, and God's voice calling me in unique ways, to understand that

I could not truly love the many, unless I could love one. After that epiphany of allowing myself to love one person, breaking through my own fears, it opened me up to love the many in a more authentic and genuine way. Loving one, truly and openly, causes us to go inward to understand, and outward to others in response to the experience. You can't find the love of one by loving the many at a distance, but you can love the many much closer, by opening yourself up to at least one other person intimately.

When I speak of loving a person intimately, it doesn't mean or is limited to a physical relationship. We can love someone intimately, and have no sexual relationship. Or we can have a sexual relationship with another, and there be no intimate love. Like many of you, I have a rather complicated relationship with sex. At times it has been confusing to me and always brings trust issues to the surface. That is okay; we are all human. The intimate love we are truly striving for is one of a sharing of hearts and souls. The experience of intimate love, with or without the physical, opens us up to our own best parts as well as to our worst.

Through this up-close and intimate relationship of love, we begin to feel uncomfortable at times as our fears surface, or our doubts begin to bubble up causing us to question, worry, or create other anxieties that only the intimacy can reveal. Loving another, or more importantly, allowing ourselves to be loved by at least one other, does bring peace and joy, but it also reveals wounds and scars that need to be healed as we will delve into in the next chapter on fears and trauma.

We can walk confidently and unknowingly through life not being aware of unconscious responses to others, until we allow

ourselves to get close to someone. Yes, love is the great uni-
fier and healer, but it is also the great unsettler and revealer. It
comes in and disrupts a comfortable existence we might have
built, and says, "You have some work to do on yourself."

Love, when shared intimately with at least one other, opens
us up to our own work we need to do, it reveals possible conflicts within us, and by this revelation unsettles us. As the Ger-
man psychologist Erich Fromm once said, "Love is a decision,
it is a judgment, it is a promise." If we can have the courage to
choose to walk through this discomfort and darkness in our own
hearts and souls, we come out the other side with a more open
and genuine love for that one and the many. And we finally are
able to allow ourselves to be loved for who we are, which is the
true test of our own courage.

How do we know love is true?

One way is when we are no longer looking for someone to
fill a hole within our own hearts. We are no longer searching
for someone to make us complete. We love not out of fear or
lack or desperate need, but we love out of our own wholeness
and abundance. We love because sharing with a person, or in a
mission for others, brings us joy and genuinely emerges out of
our authentic self. Love opens us up, and we share even more
because it is a place of plenty, not a place of scarcity where we
are grasping and grabbing out of hunger for every bit we can
like scraps.

Another way of clearly understanding love, whether it be in
an intimate connection with one, or in our purpose/mission
in the world, is really examining whether we are "all-in" with
that person, persons, or what our service is. When we have
an escape route or a safe room already built for us to quickly

retreat to, we are holding back. If we carry around a parachute in our relationships, ready to bail out at a moment's discomfort or difficulty, it raises a question about how committed we are in the small circles of life and in the large.

We will each spend a lifetime figuring out this most powerful, universal, and ancient of bonds called love. And we will love differently, and hopefully more openly, at 15, or 25, or 45, or 75. Don't beat yourself up no matter your age or place in life if you are just now discovering what you missed, or what your own insecurities hid from you. You can find love late in life, whether with a new person, or a new mission, or even a new home, and the experience of that genuine love will then help you understand how your past journey brought you to this place.

One more thing before we move on—let go of others' expectations, traditions or beliefs of what love is. Discover it on your own, through trial and error, through falling, then finding, through loss, through the long way and some short cuts, because in the end while love is a universal, its discovery is in the pointedly personal. Your compass is your heart.

Love Known

The hawks circle
In beauty and strength
Screeching out
To each other
And anyone
Who needs to hear
One speaks madly

And another responds
The wind beneath
Their wings
The water and
Cypress below
What are they saying
"This is my space"
"This is our space"
"All is okay"
"Beware of danger"
Home is like that
Words of welcome
And those of warning
Teaching children
To both trust
And be careful
To fly free
And acknowledge fear
To know you aren't lost
To know you are loved.

2
Fears and Trauma

"If you are a card-carrying human being, chances are that you share the same fear as all other humans: the fear of losing love, respect and connection to others. And if you are human, in order to avoid or prevent the pain, trauma and perceived devastation of the loss, you will do anything to avoid your greatest fear from being visited on you."

The writer, Iyanla Vanzant, had quite an inauspicious beginning to her time in this world when she was born in the back of a taxi near her family home in Brooklyn. Her father was absent most of her life, and her mother died from cancer when she was two. This quote of hers above captures so eloquently the process she went through in understanding her own fears and trauma.

It is the words and wisdom of people like Vanzant, who have seen moments of struggle, pain, and heartbreak that speak so clearly to us. We celebrate the heroes and heroines in literature or art not because of the heights they ascended or the successes they had, but we laud them for overcoming adversity. We relate to them in the most meaningful way when we understand the suffering of their lives and then their forging ahead with the hope of something better. Our heroes' humanity is built integrally in their falls and foibles and creates the connection to us as fellow human beings.

The greatest impediment to true, full love—to its acceptance within our own hearts, love for ourselves (not selfish but selfless) and then ultimately for another, and to peace within—are our fears and trauma that we have accumulated throughout our life. It is these fears and trauma, whether profoundly real or perceived, that create scars and, as a consequence, walls within us that can prevent our hearts, minds, and souls from unifying in such a way that allows us to go outward from a place of love.

In this understanding of trauma, we can also find empathy with others who might choose hate or seek to harm another. It struck me deeply not long after the gun violence at Emanuel African Methodist Church in Charleston, SC by the perpetrator Dylan Roof many of the surviving family members began to forgive him. As one family member said, "you took something very precious away from me and I will never talk to her again. I will never be able to hold her again, but I forgive you." Without some bond of love in their life and some light of warmth and connection, they know no other place than one of fear. And lacking the true loving connection on some level somewhere, they band together in a place of hate with others who also are searching for deep affection. Sadly, without the light of love, they then pursue burning others down as the only light they know.

Often the question posed is what comes first—our fears or our trauma? The answer is that it is likely both.

Sometimes our fears come first. We might be in an environment or a situation where our fear is real and justified; we clearly and genuinely sense some impending hardship, abuse or danger. The trauma that we are afraid of might not have actually occurred, but our fear signals to us that it is likely. We then begin to erect barriers to try to protect ourselves. If we operate for any lengthy period of time in this space of fear, this in itself can become a scar and a trauma fully on its own even if the actual trauma we feared never occurred.

Other times the trauma comes unexpectedly. Someone we love or we believe is supposed to love us, seemingly out of nowhere, does something that hurts us. And that hurt can be physical, emotional, or soulful. And from that unexpected trauma, fear begins to seep into our hearts and psyche. We erect walls in its aftermath, both consciously and unconsciously, in order to protect ourselves from further abuse of some kind. And even when we hate, we are using that as a protection mechanism because we are afraid to encounter additional trauma.

We build up these walls because we are responding to what we, at the very least, perceive as reasonable fears, and genuine trauma in our life. We believe this brick-by-brick wall we construct will protect us, and often in the short term it does. It seems to quiet our anxieties, settle our nerves, and give us a safe space to at least reside momentarily. It allows us some time to rest, process, or be at some semblance of peace. But it also gets in the way of seeing the adverse effects of trauma and the fears associated with our pain.

Once those fears and trauma are embedded within us, we begin to make decisions, often without even thinking the steps through, unconsciously or subconsciously, that we believe or intuitively sense will allow us to keep pain or trauma from happening again and again. If we don't take the time to analyze and look closely at what is driving us, we spend years, or even a lifetime, allowing our fears and trauma to hold the steering wheel of our decision-making especially where it concerns intimacy or how close we allow people to get to us. And by doing that, we never go all-in in our love or connection. We opt for more surface-level interaction without the depth where real love lies.

Scientists and health professionals who have studied the brain related to fear and trauma have written extensively on this topic, and so, too, have psychiatrists and psychologists from Sigmund Freud to Carl Jung to Mary Ainsworth. And they all have explained the consequences of the long-term effects of trauma and how fear gets into our bodies and shuts us off from genuine feeling and trust. As the Dutch psychiatrist Bessel A. van der Kolk wrote in his book *The Body Keeps Score: Brain, Mind and Body in the Healing of Trauma*, "Traumatized people chronically feel unsafe inside their bodies: The past is alive in the form of gnawing interior discomfort. Their bodies are constantly bombarded by visceral warning signs, and, in an attempt to control these processes, they often become expert at ignoring their gut feelings and in numbing awareness of what is played out inside. They learn to hide from their selves."

I am quite sure, even without reading all the science on this area, we have an intuitive sense of the damages and dangers of fear and trauma in our lives. We may have even told ourselves a story of survival through this trauma and why we might be justified in acting the way we do in our relationships and our communities. We build up a myth that we are the heroes of our own story of grit and resilience. In part that is true because we have journeyed through some of the worst stuff. But in another way, the story we tell ourselves is a way to justify not ever getting too close to another.

The scars created from our fears and trauma are real even if we don't take the time to look at them clearly or spend time in introspection to uncover them. These scars are there, not far beneath the surface, waiting to be poked by something in our life. Do we strongly overreact to what we perceive as a slight in our life? Do we play a cat and mouse game of "come closer, go away" in our relationships? Do we look for any opportunity to find some way someone we are in a relationship with broke our trust, so we can say, "Aha, I knew it?" Do we unknowingly, consistently choose people for relationships who are, in fact, untrustworthy so that we are confirmed in our belief system when all goes wrong?

Something we should consider is that it isn't only individuals that retain fears and trauma. Groups of people can have fears that bind them together in their mutual suffering from the trauma, and again this can be real or perceived. Organizations can be trapped in a fear and trauma cycle. And even countries can suffer a trauma that affects how they interact with fellow citizens or make governing decisions.

In America today, as we have in our past—with the genocide committed against Native Americans, the Civil War, the Great Depression, and so many other violent wars—we are in the midst of either continuing to suffer trauma, and experience fear, or we are trying to move on in the aftermath of a traumatic time. For many in this country, the trauma has been real regardless of your political persuasion. There has been an assault on our way of life and our democratic norms in how we engage with one another.

This trauma today stretches from the millions of families affected by the losses from the Coronavirus, a complete change in our way of life and connections, the trauma our planet is suffering from due to climate change, the abusive behaviors of our highest leaders in both discourse and displays of hatred, and an economy that a majority are struggling on a day-to-day basis. Real fears have risen in this moment, genuine trauma is being suffered by our country, and this has all embedded its way into the body politic. We must understand this if we are to make decisions clearly and not respond unconsciously to what we have suffered.

And through this trauma, fear causes us to question what is next, how will things be in the future, and what walls we need to erect to guard one another from even more trauma. For many of us, the trauma has become so intertwined in us that we can't even engage rationally with one another. We jump to conclusions way too quickly, and we can overreact to anything we perceive as a journey back to that trauma.

Like individuals who have made a conscious decision to love differently and more authentically and who have the courage to do the work of uncovering, examining, and healing wounds, we as a country must do the same. Before we can move forward as a nation and rebuild relationships, we must address this trauma and heal. Healing isn't about getting someone else to do something differently or pointing the finger at another group as they're needing fixing, but instead looking within, understanding our fears, and knocking down the walls we have built up that keep us from where we truly are meant to be and from living up to our highest purpose.

My experience in life has opened my heart up to a fundamental truth in this area. Having suffered my own trauma in various moments of my time on this Earth, and having done a ton of work to reduce my barriers to intimacy and connection, I see that nearly every decision we make in life is made either out of fear or out of love. It took a ton of my own personal introspection through both spiritual and secular readings on the causes and effects of trauma, as well as working with therapists and counselors to delve even deeper into my brokenness. Think about all the key decisions in your life, and strip them all down to the basics, and you might find the truth of this as well.

And even consider the great leaders in history in whatever field they might have been in, from politics to spirituality to economics to sports; more often than not, the leaders we respect and admire the most are those who often made decisions and led from a place of love as opposed to fear, and they didn't allow the trauma suffered to unconsciously guide them.

Like the process of deepening our love, it is almost always in a place of quiet and contemplation that we eventually get in touch with and process our fears and trauma. It is so easy to fill our lives with cursory interactions, be on social media constantly, turn on the television, or invite a whole gathering of people over because we know when we sit calmly and quietly alone, the trauma and fears will arise, and with them pain and hurt that we haven't fully overcome. As has been often said, the only way to the other side, isn't around, but through.

However, we can choose not to just wallow in our hurts and stay in a place of sadness or cynicism. In order to get through, we absolutely need a real hope that there is something better, more joyful and peaceful as we cross the turbulent sea of trauma. For myself, creating a vision of how I could feel on the other side, and what it would look like was absolutely key for me getting through it all in a way that fears lessened, and love grew.

I have spoken and written in the past about my oldest son's military service in his deployments in the midst of the war in Iraq, and it is meaningful to reflect on his fears and my fears as he served his country. My fear as a father, and I am sure his mother and his siblings, too, was that he would get shot or bombed by an improvised explosive device, that he would come home seriously injured or not come home at all. I would fall asleep each night in fear, hoping the next day wouldn't bring unwelcome news in confirmation of that fear.

My son's fear, as he expressed to me before he deployed, as I helped him pack his bag, was that he would have to shoot an enemy combatant or, even worse, an innocent civilian who might happen to be in the wrong place at the wrong time, and he knew how harmful that would be to his own heart and psyche. Too many soldiers come home after battle with some of their worst fears confirmed, and they suffer incredible trauma. But one thing we need to keep in mind is that trauma extends not just to those who have been injured but to those who might have been required to injure the enemy on the battlefield.

Thankfully, my worst fears about my son did not come to fruition, and neither did his. He never had to shoot anyone while he was in Iraq. Other soldiers are not nearly as fortunate, and they come back home with fears exacerbated and/or with debilitating posttraumatic stress. And we all know the work ahead they have, requiring the help of so many, in re-entering civilian life. And that is another inspiration for us to push forward and choose to work on our own traumas and fears, even if our battles are not military, but ones we encounter right here in our homes or in our communities.

There are many people in your life that have done this work, who can be Sherpas on the way up a mountain you perceive as Everest. Something to consider as we walk through life is that everyone carries with them some pain or trauma that we have no clue about. I remember walking out of the hospital after my daughter passed away, while her twin sister sat on life's edge inside, and passing people by in the store or on the street and thinking they had no idea what I was going through. How could they? And I remember that experience as I see people today in the mundane tasks of life. It must drive us to compassion as we are likely unaware of what the person changing our oil or checking us out at the grocery store is going through or has suffered. We each have a story of pain, heartache, and wounding, and it is in the telling of that story to oneself that one begins to heal. We can simultaneously help heal and give direction to others by first developing a deeper vision of and empathy for one another.

We are all born unique, and we each are different in so many ways, but there is at least one thing we have in common—we have joys and sorrows we each have experienced and thus share. We each have had and have fears. We each have gone through trauma of some kind. We each have experienced moments of real joy—falling in love, the birth of a child, or a moment of beauty standing in nature or in front of a great work of art.

Let us share more of those sorrows and joys with one another, and we can make steps toward making decisions not out of fear, but out of some abiding love. Let us turn the trauma of our lives from a tragedy into a comedy. And though it seems a paradox, both spending time alone to acknowledge our wounds, and time with others who are making their way through is the only way I know of getting out of our own way to happiness. Serving others who are in the midst of trauma, whatever it might be, is a great way to repair our own damaged hearts.

And in an interesting way, this same prescription is true for our country in the trauma it has suffered. Even as our political tribes look across the canyon of division when we think we have nothing in common, or in the justice system where sides have gone to their corners, or in the economics of inequality, we can begin the process of healing by understanding each other's joys and sorrows.

It is there we can begin to rebuild and reform our country and communities. Before you venture toward a political discussion, build a connection of heart based on shared joy and sorrow we have all been through in the paths we have walked. And maybe in some shared sense of national service, we can create more unity even through all the diversity of America.

Yes, my fears and trauma have been a part of me, and have left some scarring. Those scars are real, as are yours. And we each have done yeoman's work to this point, as best we could, in surviving what can be a difficult and tragic life on this planet. And now we are ready for something more. We are now ready to begin removing the bricks in the walls that we constructed to protect us from further pain and trauma.

And it is so important to remember struggle, pain and trauma on their own don't educate us and grow us and evolve us to be better people. We must explore the suffering in conjunction with other values and in a place of compassion for ourselves and others. As the writer Anne Morrow Lindbergh wrote in her work *Gift from the Sea*, "I do not believe that sheer suffering teaches. If suffering alone taught, all the world would be wise, since everyone suffers. To suffering must be added mourning, understanding, patience, love, openness, and the willingness to remain vulnerable."

We will each have great fear and hesitation in beginning the process to dismantle the walls that kept us safe in so many ways, but I can promise you there is a meadow and a sunrise on the other side that will astound you. Know that as you were born with the courage to originally build the wall in the face of rough and tough circumstances, so, too, it also means you have the courage to decide you no longer need that wall and you have the strength to knock it down.

Present in Pain

Sun shining bright
A breeze gently blows
Jumping on a bike
To ride for calm
Turning a corner too fast
A mind distracted
Hitting a rut
And tumbling down
Scrapes and bruises
Pain and blood
A stranger stops
And helps out of caring
Brush myself off
Gingerly ride home

Lying in bed
Smiling at the help
Done for no reason
Sheets touch the wounds
Sharp pain apparent
Makes one present
In a moment of feeling
A lesson learned
To feel
Whether bad or good
Is to be here
Without a moment
To waste.

3
Past, Present, Future

"I will honour Christmas in my heart, and try to keep it all the year. I will live in the Past, the Present, and the Future. The Spirits of all Three shall strive within me. I will not shut out the lessons that they teach."

Ebenezer Scrooge speaks these words and conveys this profound truth in the culmination of Charles Dickens' tale of redemption, "A Christmas Carol," a story published in 1843 about changing our life in the present in order to be more kind in our future. It's a tale that the reader (or watcher on television) knows is a ghost story, and it is a fundamental explanation of reality and the ghosts we all live with each day.

Like today in America, England of Dickens' time was going through wrenching change and societal disruption. London was in the midst of the Industrial Revolution, there was growing economic turmoil and income inequality, and the health of the population, especially children, was suffering from the effects of rampant pollution and disease. So Dickens, through his Christmas tale, was advocating for transformational change of not only the individual, but for society as a whole.

The words of Dickens reveal to me—and hopefully all of us—a compelling lesson in many areas of life, personal, professional and political. Each of us, when we watch movies, listen to music or read books, starts out in a place of merely sitting and passively enjoying the experience right in front of us, and then something speaks to us in a larger and deeper way. A truth that sets our mind wondering, our heart wandering, and our soul yearning for meaning.

Often, when we read inspirational or spiritual works, it is said we must stay in the present in order to appreciate what is right in front of us, and it will provide us a place of peace. So many people of wisdom through the years, in writing and spoken word, have given us this sage advice of staying in the moment now, being in the present as much as we can, and not looking backward or projecting forward. The advice is intended to give us peace and calm, and settle us as we are told that the only thing real is the present.

We hear this extending from the wisdom of Buddha—"Do not dwell on the past, do not dream of the future, concentrate the mind on the present moment"—to Thich Nhat Hanh— "To live in the present moment is a miracle. The miracle is not to walk on water. The miracle is to walk on the green earth in the present moment, to appreciate the peace and beauty that are available now"—to the modern spiritual teacher Eckhart Tolle—"The only thing that is ultimately real about your journey is the step that you are taking at this moment. That's all there ever is."

Yes, these wise words are true and helpful, though they are not the entire truth and might confuse you as they do me sometimes. For instance, what do we do about our past, and what do we plan or envision for our future? As we strive to be present, what responsibility do we have for decisions we made in the past? What do we do with harm we have suffered, harm others have suffered, or harm we have caused?

Our past has created who we are through all those experiences that filled our heart or broke it. We made past decisions that possibly helped others at times or hurt someone at other times. We have made friends, adversaries or even enemies in our past who may or may not be friends, adversaries or enemies in our present. We ended relationships or marriages that entangled our lives with another's, and there may still be an intertwining involving children, our professions or our finances.

We do have to acknowledge our past and accept it, and in some cases, we bear some present responsibility for past decisions that may continue to need our attention. Even if we want to forget about certain things in our past, and fully embrace the present, the interconnectedness of our past may require work in our present in ways we must be accountable for. And sometimes our past informs decisions we make about our future.

This does not mean we don't let go and move on, but letting go and moving on does not preclude retaining some obligations for last month's, last year's or last decade's decisions we made. And just because we might have "moved on" doesn't necessarily mean someone else has done the same in the same way. This could be someone who is no longer in our life, or who may still be in our life in a fundamentally different way, or who we wish was in our life. Our past relationships, with all their complications and complexities, may carry present responsibility or have future implications.

My past of growing up in Michigan in a rather dysfunctional family of 11 children can prevent me from being fully in the present. I carry my role designated in that large family as the third in birth order, along with scars that occurred in my youth with me today. And those interactions of the past, along with still being part of a large family today, never fully are left behind as just the past. My two marriages, with children involved, and my subsequent two divorces will be with me until my last breath. Though relationships adapt and change through the years, the steps in the past affect my footprint in the present. My various places of work and purpose in the past often crop up in my activities today, in some ways helpful and in some ways not.

And even as we process our past, and move forward, others whom we have touched have their own version of the past, and their own process of dealing with it, whether we engage with that person or not today. No matter how we stay in the present, we know we have a past. The past is never completely gone even if it is forgotten by us or others who have crossed our paths or might come into our life in the present or the future.

By staying in the present, do we create a vision for the future we desire for ourselves or others? Do we make plans so that steps can be taken toward that future? Do we let a future we are hungry for influence what we do in the present? Should our ideas and dreams about the future come into the present and occupy some mind and heart space?

The answer to all of these is yes, even if it is paradoxical. And one revelation which came to me that now seems very clear is that truth is most often found in the paradox. No matter how hard we twist the world and try to see things as black and white, reality always tells us to look at the shades. And we realize in sitting in the present of the paradox of truth, in looking back on the truth of the past, we can chart a future of integrity. The last few years have shown us the crucial importance of pursuing truth even if it is a paradox. We know this in our own lives as we repair damage done by not being true or failing to honor truth, and we also see the disastrous consequences of leaders who haven't used the truth as a guiding light.

From the Flint, Michigan, lead water crisis, to the Covid pandemic, and to the conspiracy theories surrounding the election with untruths told about voter fraud, we see the harmful effects when leaders are dishonest with citizens and not transparent about what is known and unknown. It harmed people, it harms our democracy, it breaks people's faith and hope in others, and it fractures the love our fellow men and women are so desperately hungry for. We must incorporate the past in conjunction with our present so we don't repeat the same mistakes in the future.

The hope, faith and love we want to embrace in our present are absolutely connected to our hope, faith and love in the future. We can stay fully in the present on a hike in nature up a hillside at each step, but part of the joy in the walk is that we have a goal or a dream of seeing the world from the summit where the trail we are taking leads. Also, if on that trail we took some missteps or wrong turns as we look back, it certainly will affect the route we take to the summit in the present.

We will definitely have struggles and difficulties in the present, but part of being able to shoulder the burdens is our vision of a brighter future. If we have experienced the heartbreak of the loss of a relationship in life, part of the healing moving forward is the capacity to hope and dream of a time when our heart is full again. We may lose a job, and seriously worry about what will happen to us or our family, and the vision of another place of employment or opening a business of our own, gives us the energy and drive to get up every day to move forward, to keep pursuing and actively searching, and allows us to achieve some peace in this moment at hand.

In sports, there is the same need for having a future firmly planted in one's heart and mind in order to move through a difficult present. An athlete who wants to come back after a setback like an injury needs a vision of the future of playing again in the big game or running in the next race or getting back on the ice, which gives them strength through recovery and rehabilitation. Sports franchises themselves can't effectively go through the hardship of rebuilding without clearly seeing the team playing at some point in the championship game.

Think about the golfer Tiger Woods—a superstar in his sport and an incredibly flawed human being. He personifies the understanding of past, present and future, and the perseverance through damage and hardship, some physically and emotionally inflicted on him, and some caused to others in his life and sport. And he now faces additional hardship and recovery after being seriously injured once again, this time in an early morning car accident in California which is likely to be a complicated story of its own.

From a very young age, Woods was looked at as the future of his sport. So much so that he had very little time to be a child in his present. He was pushed, and he pushed himself daily, to be the greatest golfer. He became the best: winning trophy after trophy, receiving accolades like no other, and being celebrated as possibly the greatest golfer ever. And then through physical injury and reckless personal decisions, he fell from his position on top of the world dramatically. Hardly anyone thought

Woods could recover from these tragic circumstances and win again, and many thought he would never golf again. And then in 2019 he won his fifth Masters and fifteenth major title. He did this by striving in the present, relying on the past success and lessons learned from his mistakes, and to a measurable degree by creating a vision of the future of once again wearing the Green Jacket.

Golf to me has become an exercise in embracing the past, present, and future as I walk the fairways. Anyone in golf sets a goal for what they want on the hole (the future) and the path they will take to get the ball into the hole. We know if we mess up the shot in the present, that now past event will affect not only our possible score but also the path we take to the green. And every golfer knows that for that brief moment of standing over the ball, we must let go of the past and put the future out of our minds, and stay in the present for the swing. Golf may not be your hobby, but if you are a runner, or a gardener, or even a weekend chef you know as well the lessons of interweaving past, present and future to simultaneously achieve peace and success.

The powerful paths of historical change and advancements of humanity all point to the absolute crucial necessity of having a vision of the future. So many of the key freedom movements in history trying to right injustices of the past, and experiencing violence in the present, found the only way to manage through a traumatic time was to see and feel a future ahead. Think of the civil rights movement here in America. As people were beaten, abused, and discriminated against for decades, they were only able to overcome by having hope of getting to the mountaintop. They had to be rooted in the promise of receiving justice at some point in the future, the dream that life would be more fair and equal. Any movement to independence of a country, through all the fights and battles, had to have a vision of the future that gave the participants faith and fortitude in the present of their struggle.

Even superstar celebrity, entertainer, writer, and philanthropist Oprah Winfrey seems to have lived out this idea of understanding simultaneously the past, present and future. Oprah was born into poverty in rural Mississippi to a single teenage mom, and she not only used it as a jumping off point in her drive for changing her own circumstances, but she also uses and honors her humble and difficult beginnings as she pushes to empathize with and bring change to other people's lives.

Oprah talks regularly to philosophers and spiritual writers and leaders about the need to stay in the present, while she never forgets the past that came before now. And her motivation is to try to inform people how they can change their future by constructing a vision of where they might want to go. On a visit one day to her beautiful Montecito home with panoramic views, I reflected in conversation with her about her vision. I quoted to her a scene from the miniseries Lonesome Dove. In it, at the very end, a local reporter says to Woodrow Call, played by Tommy Lee Jones, "They say you're a man of vision. Is that true?" Call flashes back to his whole life, and finally responds, "Yeah. Hell of a vision." For Oprah to come from where she came from in the past, as she teaches in the present and creates beauty around her, she had to be a woman with a "hell of a vision."

Reflect for a moment on your own path. On the past that made you who you are and a past that had hurdles that you had to overcome, or people that you still have responsibility for in your present. Sit in your present and be at peace, and pause long enough to be clear about your vision. I have a story of past, present and future, as do each of you. And my story, or Oprah's story or Tiger Woods' story is no more significant than yours. We each are different, and being clear about our story can help us understand ourselves, and ultimately others.

Dickens was incredibly wise in his story of keeping the ghosts of past, present and future in our hearts. He seemed to have intuitively understood the necessity of all three as we attempt to live our lives fully with meaning, purpose and personal responsibility. The path to redemption and transformation of us as human beings isn't just about staying in the present as wonderful and wise people often suggest, but about building a solid stool of peace and purpose whose three legs are the past, present and the future.

The story of one's own journey through the past, present and future is not just a tale unveiling truth in a personal relationship, it is also a tale with a lesson for our country and the world. Usually, every revelatory insight we achieve at the micro level personally, has a window of truth to a macro level.

We often ask ourselves, "What does my little insignificant story have to say about the world as a whole?" Every story of our battles and victories, our own struggles and triumphs, and our both simple and complicated relationships at a personal level underscore every broader story of the world. Think about the deeper meaning of what is going on in your life today, and one realizes that the truth of one's own life tells a truth that spans the globe. What you see in your home and around your hearth reveals what the dynamics are in our bigger world.

With regard to that dynamic, nations must also wrestle with their pasts as its people make decisions in the present, and begin to fashion a future for their country through a shared vision. And in America today this is crucial. We could use a mutual vision of what we want our country to stand for, and what as a country the values are that we all agree on to move forward in the present in a more harmonious way. Yes, there are deep divides, injustice and trauma that have been in our past, and at some point we will need to delve into the differences; but to heal, let us come together in the present with shared heartfelt connections, and begin to agree on a shared vision.

It is often important to remind ourselves of our past, both as individuals and a country, in order for us to accept truths and responsibility, and know the present or future of peace isn't possible without repairing damage already done. This is a difficult process for anyone or any country, and the way forward is to embrace a shared vision of the future. We must see ourselves in the big game ahead if we are to go through the tough process of rebuilding or rehabilitating in the present.

For those of us who speak from a place of faith, sometimes it seems easier to find the hope for a better future and manage the struggles through the difficulties of our daily lives. However, faith doesn't necessarily have to have religious underpinnings. It could be about believing in something bigger than ourselves, or in being aware of the basic goodness of life and each other and that in the long expanse of history, others were successful in the path of enlightenment.

We can see our own lives as a series of festivities and joys of an ongoing holiday celebration. A daily holiday where the gift we give ourselves or each other isn't something bought online or at a store, but in a shared acceptance and understanding of the mystery of life and the idea that time is a construct with divisions that don't truly exist.

And then we each can carry the spirts of the Past, Present and Future in a manner that renews our own ideals and gives us peace in our own lives and as a country or larger community of folks. Let us be present for ourselves and those we love, but also know our present is composed of our past which hungers for resolution, and our present is also made more beautiful and bearable by a future we can see and then move forward toward.

A River Rises

The rains come
Creeks fill
Off barren land
Water cascades
To a river white
Of limestone bottom
Quickly rises
Over pasture of green
Carrying debris
Accumulated over time
Piles of brush
And of trees fallen
Swept down with the current
As force moves strongly
Rains subside
And water retreats
To its natural path

Leaving behind
Remnants of strangers
Upstream swept here
And what was here is gone
What was there is left
Another day
Of memories past
And newness present
With future to come

4

Ends and Means

"They say 'means are after all means.' I would say 'means are after all everything.' As the means so the end...There is no wall of separation between means and end. Indeed the Creator has given us control (and that too very limited) over means, none over the end. Realization of the goal is in exact proportion to that of the means. This is a proposition that admits of no exception."

These words of Mahatma Ghandi, written in what has been called his paper or journal *Young India* in 1924, might give us a better direction than other renowned "wise" folks who are way too frequently quoted by leaders in politics and business. Ghandi, who once wore the garb of Western accomplishment and ultimately adopted the "loin cloth" of the poor, in pursuit of his goal (or end) of Indian independence from the British Empire, put in place the successful strategy and means of non-violent non-cooperation. I would suggest his way is not only more just, but more successful toward real change in our life than the other two historical figures oft repeated and mirrored.

In 1513, philosopher Niccolò Machiavelli released the book *The Prince*, where, though he didn't write the exact words, he espoused the sentiment of the "ends justify the means." Mach-iavelli's work, along with the Chinese treatise *The Art of War* by Sun Tzu, have become the mainstay of an unfortunate num-ber of people and leaders today. It has become commonplace to pursue the idea of winning at all costs, to pursue whatever means and acts to achieve victory, as if following the ideas of writers from centuries ago should control our interactions with others, or even worse, how we treat ourselves.

Too often in our lives, as well as in our politics and our com-munities, we follow this philosophy laid out by Machiavelli—that the ends justify the means. To achieve some desired end or goal, we pursue whatever means will allow us to attain it, regardless of the damage done in the meantime, or the corrup-tion of our country or community. And in the end, this path corrupts our own souls for the sake of achievement of some result.

We pursue more money or positions or a place in the world as the driving force of what we do each day. In the pursuit of what seems flashy or important, we compromise our own held values and cast a shadow on our own hearts. We neglect our connections and the bonds we each share, and at moments, we even sacrifice the most valuable and most nonrenewable resource in life, which is the time we have, to get to some finish line that we have stretched across a road in our minds.

Political campaigns, and leadership in general, are run and policies pushed that we believe are for the good of the com-munity or country in a manner that leaves important values neglected and broken. This has become especially apparent over the last few years. Disrespecting others, dividing us into hateful tribes, adopting mean-spirited and hateful ways, and treating integrity and honesty as naive seems like the norm, and in some circles, it is actually cheered and rewarded. Once we employ malicious or shallow means to an end, we all suffer in the process.

It is time we forget Machiavelli and Sun Tzu, let them gather dust on library bookshelves, along with so many other comparable philosophers, and realize that power or wins gained through illicit or short-sighted means leave us all lost in this world. It takes away our peace, and we are in a constant battle in the circles of our worlds. It leaves us hungry for something other; it leaves the bonds we share frayed, or worse, torn completely apart.

Let us turn this ends-justify-the-means approach 180 degrees on its head, and move toward a means-justify-the-ends way of life. These philosophers of old, whether Machiavelli or espousers of the same principle, had the words right, they just had them in the wrong order. War is never an art, but a destruction of the truth of what beauty and meaning in art is supposed to be for our souls.

Looking at the expanse of civilization, we can be assured that if the means are good, if they are based on love and engaging all with dignity, then the ends will work out as they should. It is conceiving of and practicing the proper means that must be the driving force of our path. And trusting that if our means are heartfelt and soulful, we can trust the ends will build our connections and be in the interest of the common good. Putting peaceful relationships ahead of gains through warring factions will allow us to bring a real sense of community to fruition.

As a Christian, I was reflecting on all of this after chapel one Sunday at a non-denominational Church here in Central

Texas called Chapel in the Hills. Jesus advocated throughout the Gospels for a means-justify-the-ends philosophy, and he definitely would be the polar opposite of Machiavelli and Sun Tzu. Jesus was all about the means. He believed that if we loved each other and treated one another equally and with respect and dignity, including our enemies (talk about a radical and revolutionary command!), then we would be establishing the Kingdom of God here in our midst. His command and strategy were that we could create that kingdom not in some far off place or at the end of our life, but right here and right now.

Jesus' constant and consistent ministry was focused on treating strangers decently and with compassion, welcoming the outcasts, forgiving those who trespass against us, feeding the hungry, and loving one another. As Brennan Manning writes in his book *The Ragamuffin Gospel: Good News for the Bedraggled, Beat-Up, and Burnt Out*, "The kingdom is not an exclusive, well-trimmed suburb with snobbish rules about who can live there. No, it is for a far larger, homelier, less self-conscious caste of people who understand they are sinners because they have experienced the yaw and pitch of moral struggle."

Jesus didn't say if you want to get to heaven, do this. He said do this, and heaven will be here on Earth. His parable of the Good Samaritan was all about the means and how we interact with one another regardless of biography or background. It wasn't about sticking with artificial rules or with moving fast through life to get to our destination, but it was about stopping along the way and tending to others.

Rather than just seeing this as the bigger picture, we each might look at it as the small steps we make in our daily life.

I often get impatient if I am stuck in traffic and need to get somewhere fast. Or I get upset or irritated if I am waiting in line at the store and somebody in front of me is taking too long. We might honk at someone or raise our voice trying to convey we don't have time for this because we need to get somewhere. We focus on the end we want, and lose touch with the means of having a positive personal calm interaction and moment we are in.

When I came back years ago from a spiritual trek to experience different faiths in the world, one of the things that struck me was the disorganization and chaos in parts of India, and that nearly everyone there accepted the noise, traffic jams and constant disruption as they went about their daily lives. They seemed to accept it all with patience and didn't get upset or fight angrily against what was happening around them even if it delayed what they were doing. They even just ignored cows lazily walking across streets and walkways, and moved along when the coast was clear.

When I got back home to Central Texas, I had this feeling of peace that would give me pause in all my rushing around. I thought to myself, if folks in India could be at ease with so much less in resources and so much more in hassles, then why shouldn't I. And why was I in a hurry anyway? What was I really rushing to do, or what was it so important I had to get to at the end of a trip around town? It spurred me to ask questions about the means and meaning of each day. Today, I am flawed and don't always remember this lesson from India, and I even get impatient with my impatience.

What brings us peace and joy on a daily basis? What makes us feel in harmony with others or with our own heart? Being kind, patient and calm, and letting go of the attachment of our ends or the desired results. Seeing others with inherent respect and dignity, and knowing that a kind word, act, or even subtle smile and quiet energy can fundamentally change a situation. Once we settle into the means of our interactions and being present compassionately, we ultimately achieve the ends we truly want—a pursuit of happiness and a less stressful existence.

Many in life, whether in politics or corporate America, or in simple decisions in our neighborhoods, want to win so badly, they discard the values they raise their children with, and accept behaviors that are unethical or unacceptable. We too often look at the world as some sort of game with points scored, chips accumulated, and win/loss records highlighted. And too often commentators on television cover life in this manner, as if we're all separated into teams who are opponents on the field.

Some citizens of this country see an opponent or an opposing tribe as a danger, and want it removed by any means necessary. While I understand this view, conducting our lives and politics in a way that harms our relationships will only make matters worse in the long term. Allowing our country and communities and our meaningful relationships to devolve into hate, competitions for power, and anger-filled groups or tribes will do incredible damage, and though we might win in the short term, we will break all the bonds that bind us together in our common humanity...not an end anybody wants.

Yes, we must clearly point out the truth, battle for justice, and look out for others who are harmed in the process. But let us use love to conquer hate, let us win with integrity, let us put peace before war, and let us not forget the spark of the divine that resides in each of us. It is only then that we can transform our own world and the whole world for the better.

And truth is an interesting concept in this means and ends discussion. Yes, I believe in being honest wherever possible, and telling the truth as a basic fundamental tenet of the way to live life and relate to one another. But just like ends, there is a hierarchy of means; at times we must choose the higher means over other means that we value.

Is not being honest to save a life wrong? If our grandparent or our child is threatened, is it okay to mislead or even say something that is not true? I believe yes, because love is a more important motive and action than the letter of the law of being specifically honest in a certain situation or scenario. We must be very careful here, however, and really examine our motive and our means when we are sacrificing one fundamental value for a higher one. Lying to save our position or hiding something out of personal interest (we don't want to be discovered that we did something wrong or harmful to another) is putting self-interest as the end goal, and not love of another.

Is it ever okay to break the law? History tells us that at times when justice is at stake, breaking the law becomes a necessity in achieving a just society. The means in this instance is practicing justice, and not merely avoiding getting arrested or being held accountable by some civil authority. The civil rights movement in America was built in many steps of confronting civil authority in order to highlight means of injustice in our communities.

In his essay "Civil Disobedience," Henry David Thoreau wrote about this as he states, "Unjust laws exist; shall we be content to obey them, or shall we endeavor to amend them, and obey them until we have succeeded, or shall we transgress them at once?" Mahatma Gandhi practiced this as he sought to bring freedom and justice to his native India. And Martin Luther King, Jr. ended up jailed in Birmingham, Alabama, as he confronted discrimination and abuse in American society. King wrote a famous letter from that jail where in part he states, "One has not only a legal, but a moral responsibility to obey just laws. Conversely, one has a moral responsibility to disobey unjust laws." Each of these leaders knew the means of justice was more important than the ends of being a law-abiding citizen in all circumstances.

Again, this approach must be thoughtful and meaningful in its unfolding, and we each must examine our own consciences when we begin to put in place a hierarchy of means in how we make decisions, as well as the means we employ in conjunction with the ends we are confronting. We also must be willing to be held accountable and accept the punishment as we build a more just society and fight for the idea that all are created equal. If we practice levels of civil disobedience in a fight for equality, we must be willing to peacefully accept the accountability of laws and regulations.

In this world, and in our own personal worlds, a life lived where the means of love and peace are preeminent isn't without sacrifice and struggle. It may mean reconstituting relationships in our life, it may include ending commitments we have made because keeping them causes us to practice means which aren't true to our hearts, or it may mean leaving jobs that aren't in line with our values, or living a more simple life that allows us to live the means in a more clear and uncomplicated way.

Putting the means before the ends doesn't require a religious life. In fact, there are far too many people who follow some fundamental approach to religion who are some of the worst practitioners of the ends-justify-means philosophy of life. They harm others, whether intentionally or unintentionally, because they think they will achieve some higher end in the afterlife by doing so. And an atheist can be one of the most authentic followers of the vision of Jesus Christ in his or her means-justify-the ends compassionate ways.

It is important to keep in mind as we look to a life of living good means and letting go of the ends that one doesn't have to believe in God to have ethics or lead a moral life. Too many religious folks try to mandate the idea that a person has to accept the existence of God to be able to choose between right and wrong. Through history, and practiced by many citizens today, there is something called secular morality. And it has been alive and well for thousands of years, and it is the way a large segment of the world lives.

To live a virtuous life does not require religion or a belief in God. And interestingly, there are times people's religious tenets get in the way of choosing means like compassion and justice because the religious rules demand some pattern of behavior in conflict with humanity at times. While religion or faith can help provide direction for those of us who are followers, it certainly isn't determinative of morality or the lack of a moral standard. As famed atheist, writer, philosopher and neuroscientist Sam Harris has written, "Indeed, religion allows people to imagine that their concerns are moral when they are highly immoral— that is, when pressing these concerns inflicts unnecessary and appalling suffering on innocent human beings."

I have often described myself as either religious or spiritual and have been as long as I can remember. In fact, my earliest memory I can recall in life was when I was three years old at

Christ the King Church in Detroit, Michigan. I was at Mass sitting next to my mom when I noticed a small ball of dust under the kneeler. I thought to myself, that doesn't belong in church. I picked it up in my small hands and looked around to see what I should do with it. I looked up at the guy in charge at the front of the church dressed in a fancy way, praying and talking with us, and decided I needed to bring it to him.

I walked out of the pew and slowly and carefully made my way down the aisle between the pews, and I could feel all the congregants staring at me. I walked all the way up to the altar and handed the dust to the priest, and then turned around and walked back next to my mom. She smiled and patted my shoulder. It seems I somehow knew at a young age that the means of church and my small attempt at cleaning was more important than the end of some order during Mass.

As a Christian and a Catholic, I fall short on Christ's command every day. I struggle moment to moment searching my soul to figure out the way to live out the words of the Gospels. And I have lost friends and professional relationships along the way in attempting to counter Machiavelli's philosophy in my own life and in service of a deeper and broader good. I have fallen down in so many attempts at trying to live a moral life of means.

In fact, making mistakes and then resolving to correct them is an important means we could all follow to progress toward a more moral society. Accepting that we are imperfect, that we are going to slip and fall, that we are all ragamuffins, and then getting up again and trying better and not worrying so much about judgement is one of the most meaningful means in bonding us all in a deeper way for the common good. And if we did only that, the mistakes we made would lead to a better end.

As the ancient Chinese writer and philosopher Lao Tzu purportedly once annunciated,

"Simplicity, patience, compassion. These three are your greatest treasures. Simple in actions and thoughts, you return to the source of being. Patient with both friends and enemies, you accord with the way things are. Compassionate toward yourself, you reconcile all beings in the world."

I am willing to arise each morning as the sun greets me with a new beginning, realizing that when we put the means before the ends in our lives, our politics, our economy and our personal interactions, we can live in a world where joy and peace are common. And I have faith and trust that when all is said and done, it is the means that matter far more than some ends I have conceived should happen.

White Pine

A street stands tall
Proud among pines
A symbol and signature
Of a beautiful persuasion
We all seek
Look around you
Birds sing
And rest in branches
Squirrels dance
From branch to branch

Outstretched on all sides
Embracing the air
Roots run deep
In the dirt
Of this Earth
Asking nothing
From all who enjoy
This gift of nature
And if you touch
Its rough bark
Or listen to
Its quiet voice
You can sense
Its purpose
Being the means
Not the ends
To live
And to give

5
Faith and Science

"We must accept what science tells us, that man was born from the earth. But, more logical than the scientists who lecture us, we must carry this lesson to its conclusion: that is to say, accept that man was born entirely from the world— not only his flesh and bones but his incredible power of thought."

These are the words of Pierre Teilhard de Chardin who was a scientist, a philosopher and a Jesuit priest. He embodied the seeming conflict of faith and science, and throughout his life attempted to preach and write of a more enlightened way. And though condemned by the Vatican as being out of step with Catholic Church teaching, he never lost sight of the integral part faith played in his life, and he stayed religiously devoted until his last days. He also understood his own ability to relate to ours in a positive growing way was to integrate the ways of both faith and science.

Each day for many years, I have risen in the early morning hours and read from some sacred text or religious reading (the Bible, various biographies on lives of the Saints, the Koran, Hindu or Buddhist words, etc.) as well as some informational scientific discussion on any number of various topics. I have done this as part of a morning meditation/centering prayer routine that I began over a decade ago. And I can't imagine moving out into the world without it.

After much tragedy and disruption in my life, and living from decade to decade, I realized that not only did I need a discipline in keeping my physical self healthy, I also was in dire need of a structured way to ensure my mind and soul were exercised and healthy. I had experienced the death of my mother suddenly who was discovered by a neighbor on her living room floor with a rosary in her hand. I had lost a daughter way too young, and her identical twin sister was in intensive care for nine months. And I went through my second divorce, and this for a person who never thought he would be divorced once.

I began a daily path of sitting quietly at sunrise (and often before the first morning light) and being in a place of calm and peace as I read from something that would move or inspire me. Since then, I haven't gone a day, whether traveling or at home, without taking time before the unfolding of my day began in earnest to center myself in the wise words of another. If you are so inclined and desiring the ability to be more mindful and relaxed, I recommend starting this routine in the morning before you get in the shower because as we wash up, we start to plan out our day and anticipate the stresses that await us.

So often when we simultaneously read from words of faith and words of science, we might feel in conflict. We feel the conflict of sitting in mystery that can never be proven, while also absorbing knowledge based in data and proof. And this supposed conflict is exacerbated by messages from the outside world that these two concepts cannot be aligned. In the dualistic approach of the Western world, we are pushed and prodded to pick one or the other. Too many try to force us to pick either faith or science, and align wholly with one or the other, and this either conflicts us, or confuses us.

It confuses us because there are some things deep inside us that cannot be named or described with absolute certainty. We know that science has a required level of concreteness, while faith is not rooted in facts. We have something in our soul that calls us in connection to God or whatever name we put on it, and in our minds we are taught to rely on facts and what can be readily proven. We want to delve into both, but others push us to pick one or the other.

Boxes and compartmentalization are the way of the western world, starting all the way back in ancient civilization with Plato and Aristotle and reaching up to today. However, we each are a mix of contradictions in so many different ways, and the reliance on soul, heart and mind is just one of many of those. Too often we are lectured about consistency, and not enough about balance. In our daily lives we look out at the world and demand constancy and simpler labels so we can have order amidst the chaos. We know deep down that we are an inconsistent lot, filled with contradictions, but in our jobs and our neighborhoods it is easier to place someone in a box and to categorize.

We live in a world that is composed of both facts and mystery. As discoveries are made in science, it helps solve many mysteries that people of faith found answers to in their reading or understanding of their religious tenets. Because people of faith didn't understand or were confused by the natural world, they came up with divine explanations that would allow them to have some security. Science today has explained many of those mysteries naturally, without involving the gods. However, new discoveries from the scientific world also open us to further mysteries we never knew existed before.

It wasn't that many centuries ago when men of faith began to question the idea that the sun and the other planets rotated around the Earth, and that the Earth was the center of the universe. It was determined years ago that our world was not the center, and we and other planets circled the sun. This discovery shook the religions at the time because it was in conflict with the Bible.

These discoveries were all by people who were in touch with their souls, saw themselves as religious, but also were pulled by their minds to uncover mystery in the universe. Think of Galileo, born in 1564—a pious Italian Roman Catholic, who was also a man of science and an astronomer who pushed people of his time for a clearer understanding of the sun and planets. Or consider Copernicus, born in the 15th century of what is now Poland. He had a doctorate in Church law and was also a physician and mathematician, who helped formulate a new scientific model of the universe.

The reaction of religious leaders to this science wasn't to embrace new knowledge, but to condemn these discoveries because their box of faith wouldn't allow them to open their eyes to a new way of approaching the universe. They closed their eyes to new data and information, and didn't open their minds and souls to a more expansive way of seeing their world and faith in general.

No matter where we sit or stand, we think we are the center of the universe. We look out in all directions, and we think as things stretch beyond our eyes or our comprehension that we are the center of it all. The beginnings of all religions were founded on that "we are the center" premise, and it became part of the teachings that God made us, placed planet Earth as the center, and everything else in the known universe revolved around us. Science determined this not to be true, and instead of going with knowledge, religious leaders shut their minds and tried to keep information from being disseminated.

We make this same mistake over and over; when new scientific discoveries are made, we deny or ignore the science because it doesn't go along with our preconceived notions. It is part of the human condition to overly rely on something we already thought we knew, and get very uncomfortable with new data that undermines our security in something. The discussion surrounding the effects of climate change today and the denial of the science and data by some is a distinct example.

The same happened not long ago in the elucidation of evolution and how we as humans became who we are through natural selection and the idea of survival of the fittest as illuminated by Charles Darwin. Again, faith and science confronted each other, and many in the faith community shut out science, and relied on a conception of faith that was not open to views of reality when new windows of knowledge opened. Darwin, who was baptized in the Anglican Church and regularly attended Unitarian chapel, was widely condemned and criticized by religious people in his time.

It is this inability to see both science and faith or belief systems as compatible that have created so many difficulties in our own lives and in our political institutions. I am not advocating in my understanding of faith and science that we find some "middle ground" in the resolution of the two, but rather more of a blending which has an expanded view of both God and science.

If one believes in God as an unlimited force in the universe, then why wouldn't scientific discoveries and knowledge be part of that divine plan? Why would our minds exist but to gain insights into the universe as it plays out across existence? In my own revelations of my life, the interweaving of science and faith is a paradox, which is where we ultimately find most truth. The paradox comes when faith is fundamentally about believing what we can't prove, and science is about believing only what we can prove. Being able to do both simultaneously is inherently paradoxical.

Those people of faith who shut out science and knowledge as a protective reaction of fear of it undermining their beliefs based in ancient books written by men ultimately and unfortunately make God so small and limited. Let us allow God to be bigger than we could ever envision, and when science opens our eyes in different ways, let us broaden our view of the horizon of faith. When we make God small and limited, we ultimately do this to an even greater degree to our own minds, hearts and souls.

Simultaneously, while science gives us a clear sense of the world, let us also acknowledge the more science reveals, the more we truly understand what we don't know, and allow mystery and the unknown to settle into us, which might make us more humble and open to insights gathered from diverse sources, including faith traditions.

In 1924, the conflicts of science and faith were put on public display in the Scopes Monkey Trial held in Dayton, Tennessee.

The state legislature had passed a law banning the teaching of the theory of evolution because they felt it conflicted with the Creation story of the Bible. A public school teacher decided to teach evolution in violation of the law, and thus a trial came to fruition pitting many people of faith versus people of science. And it gained national attention because of the high-profile reputations of the lawyers: William Jennings Bryan, well-known orator, populist and former Presidential candidate on the side of creationism, and Clarence Darrow, prominent American Civil Liberties Union lawyer and litigator for many high profile clients, on the side of science.

Though the school teacher and Darrow ended up losing in the moment, the publicity of the case and the arguments made ironically further advanced the cause of science and education forward, and the "faith" winners were diminished. Bryan became a laughingstock even though he won, and Darrow received considerable praise even though he lost. And more and more people began to consider the possibility of integrating the idea of faith and science, of those two major world elements being able to work together, and having all of our mutual pursuits be enlightenment. Darrow's words from years ago might ring true especially today:

"If today you can take a thing like evolution and make it a crime to teach it in the public school, tomorrow you can make it a crime to teach it in the private schools, and the next year you can make it a crime to teach it to the hustings or in the church. At the next session you may ban books and the newspapers. Soon you may set Catholic against Protestant and Protestant against Protestant, and try to foist your own religion upon the minds of men. If you can do one you can do the other. Ignorance and fanaticism is ever busy and needs feeding. Always it is feeding and

gloating for more. Today it is the public school teachers, tomorrow the private. The next day the preachers and the lectures, the
magazines, the books, the newspapers. After a while, your honor,
it is the setting of man against man and creed against creed until
with flying banners and beating drums we are marching backward to the glorious ages of the sixteenth century when bigots
lighted fagots to burn the men who dared to bring any intelli-
gence and enlightenment and culture to the human mind."

This problem of reconciling faith and science also points to a
deeper and related issue of holding onto to dogmas or ideology,
and then ignoring new information that might give us a better direction for public policy and solving some of the world's
problems. And this also affects decisions made in our economic
models where we cement ourselves into a belief system, and
we either ignore facts or we only try to find information that
confirms our locked in beliefs.

It is a natural human tendency to find security in the pre-
dictable and a structure we seem to understand, and then look
for confirmation in the world to support that structure. It is an
exceedingly uncomfortable place to accept new information that
causes us to confront a belief system we have held for a long
period of time or one that has given us direction in our lives.

The struggle over the resolution of the worldwide problem
of climate change is a perfect example of where ignoring science can have catastrophic consequences, and strict adherence
to a particular belief system doesn't allow leaders to address
the problem of man's activities' harmful effects on our globe.
This is not just some academic debate held in the halls of a
university or think tank; it unfolds in the real world for all of us
whether in droughts, floods, winter storms or hurricanes.

There is near universal agreement in the scientific community about the detrimental consequences of human behavior on the climate. What we should be arguing over is not the clear and convincing scientific facts that point out the problem, but what are the best solutions to solve the issue. Instead, because some don't accept the science, we can never get to a thoughtful debate over the proper policies.

Some denying the facts of climate change use faith as a backstop, believing somehow God will solve the problem. Or that the Bible tells these fundamental religious adherents that we can use the world for whatever we as men and women want, even if that means it is destructive to our planet. And others dispute the science, because they have a belief system that they inherently don't want objective facts to undermine because they feel it will disempower them.

As we move this conversation about faith and science out from the larger global context of policy or governance, and look at the individual circles of our own smaller worlds, we also see this playing out. So often in my own life, I ignored facts or data (the science of the interactions) revealed in a relationship because I had a belief system about someone or something. I got locked in a pattern of behavior or thought process that gave me comfort in its certainty like faith can do at times, and no matter the data and information that came along I stuck to my original beliefs.

How often have we said to ourselves about someone else we trusted that I didn't see that coming? This could be in a relationship where someone betrayed us, or overlooking telltale signs of a problem in our children's lives, or even hiring someone to do work around our house. In each instance, because of faith in some existing certainty, we missed the hints or openings of a deeper knowledge. As Peter Enns writes in his book The Sin of Certainty, "the challenges of our day-to-day existence are sustained reminders that our life of faith simply must have its center somewhere other than in our ability to build it together in our minds. Life is a pounding surf that wears away our rock-solid certainty. The surf always wins."

The same is true if we are certain in a negative perception of others. If we have had wounds in our life, or been betrayed, we close ourselves off to a new relationship of someone we might be able to trust or who is different from what we have encountered previously. Often by sticking to some locked-in belief structure, we keep picking people in our worlds who confirm this negative thought process.

If we all started from a place of greater openness, no matter if it is broad discussions about science and faith, or the resolution of a difficulty in politics, or in our small communities and families, we are much more likely to move to a more enlightened and positive place. Being open doesn't mean we don't have some principled belief system. It means we have a belief system that is open to adjustments based on new information or discovered data.

And maybe in the openness, with a bit less certainty, and the ability to adjust, we will trim our belief systems of all the small differences, and focus instead on the fundamentals that unify our world. Often times our belief systems and our faith traditions are overly tied to emotion, and it doesn't leave room for wisdom. It is so very difficult to break an emotional bond with a rational argument.

We can only allow reason in when we examine our own emotional connections. Our head—where we process science and true knowledge—is disconnected from our heart of faith and mystery because of an insecurity or vulnerability that we are likely unaware of. Once we are secure in our faith, we understand uncertainty isn't the enemy, but rather a welcome entrant to encourage a deeper faith and an expansive vision of the divine.

Mystery isn't meant to confuse us, but it is meant to question what we believe and what we know. And in that place of mystery, we can welcome both science and faith as important pillars of who we are, and how we relate to the world. Neither science nor faith has all the answers to the many mysteries of life and the universe, but an integral blending of the two is going to get us closer to the truth and our truth.

If we believe faith is a gift bestowed on us by a loving God, then we must also believe that the gift of science, knowledge and wisdom comes from the same source. Each of these areas is not some separate camp that are enemies of each other. In fact, they are allies in our exploration of the universe.

Science and faith can be at the same table, arm in arm, helping us navigate life. But we must first give up on the idea that one is the arbiter of all that is to be known. We must allow space for the unknown in the universe, and in the intimate connections of our personal life. In our search for meaning, we realize, through openness and acceptance, that as faith and science can couple, so must we integrate head, heart and soul.

A Girl and a Kite

A breeze blows
She runs with
A string in tiny hands
"Catch the breeze"

I say with assurance
There is a science
And a faith
The kite catches the wind
Lifted higher
In the clouds
I fashioned a tail
For her to keep steady
In stiff currents
Not too heavy
Which would weigh it down
Never reaching
The blue skies
"Let the string out"
So the kite can climb
Not holding too tight
So it can do
What nature commands
It flies higher and higher
A smile crosses her face
She pauses and watches
With delight and awe
Finally tired from running
She lets the kite
Land gently in a field
Confident to step forward
In another venture ahead

6
Light and Darkness

"And that's the end," she said, and she saw in his eyes, as the interest of the story died away in them, something else take its place; something wondering, pale, like the reflection of a light, which at once made him gaze and marvel. Turning, she looked across the bay, and there, sure enough, coming regularly across the waves first two quick strokes and then one long steady stroke, was the light of the Lighthouse. It had been lit."

These words of famed English writer Virginia Woolf reveal the depth of her own struggles in life as she experienced light and dark throughout her years. She lost her mother suddenly as a young teenager, and she was burdened her entire life with mental illness. Even in her times of greatest internal darkness, she managed to create light, especially in the words above taken from her novel, *To the Lighthouse*, telling the story of the Ramsay family and their treks to the Isle of Skye in Scotland.

Growing up in a large working-class family in Michigan, and having been born in Detroit, we never made it to Scotland as Woolf wrote about, but we took all our family vacations to the shores of the Great Lakes surrounding us. Usually, we would all pack into a large family station wagon, with lunch in a cooler for the trip, and try not to fight over which one of us got a window seat, or who would be smashed into the middle. And among all the yelling from our parents, the yelling at each other, and trying to get my father to stop at a restroom along the drive, we would all have great anticipation of arriving at our destination.

We would always look forward to these trips because being crowded in a house with two parents and 11 children, open space was an incredible relief, providing each of us with a rare feeling of freedom. Of course, some moments alone without having to fend off the disturbances and disruptions from others were so very welcome. And it gave us a chance to explore the world outside our small Detroit-area neighborhood and make new discoveries, even if only in the same state we lived, a few hundred miles from home. We would either rent a house or camp out (some of us preferred a solid roof for protection during regular storms), and we'd bring along only the simple necessities. We could soak up the sun, play in the water, stand on the shore and fish, collect driftwood or discover interesting stones...and nearly always nearby was a lighthouse.

On the shores surrounding the mitten of Michigan and in the Upper Peninsula are various constructions of lighthouses built through the years. Like each of us, these lighthouses come in different forms and shapes and presentations. There are "round" lighthouses, "conical" lighthouses, "skeletal" lighthouses, "pyramidal" lighthouses, and "schoolhouse" lighthouses. Some are built solidly with brick, some are made of wood, and others are more skeletal structures.

If you pay attention to the variety of lighthouses along the shore, you will find many standing pristine and tall as if they were built just yesterday. Other ones are in great need of repair, looking shabby, and having been damaged or even destroyed by the elements. As with so many structures we encounter in life, some are honored, remembered and cared for, while others are abandoned and completely let go. Some are still in use; others haven't functioned for years but still stand as a reminder of their use over the years.

I still take every opportunity to visit lighthouses whenever I can. This could be whether I am going back to see family in Michigan, walking the shores in another state, visiting the lighthouses dotting the landscape of my ancestral land of Ireland, or taking a trip directly to a lighthouse solely to gather myself and receive the peace and calm that seems to always center me when I am there. Lighthouses always convey to me a tale of meaning bigger than the building; they enhance my understanding of life and inspire me to consider how each of us might function as a "lighthouse" in our own lives.

It is speculated, with some archaeological evidence, that the first lighthouse in the world was Pharos of Alexandria, or Lighthouse of Alexandria. Built by Ptolemy II in the third century BC, having now fallen into ruin with very few remains discovered, it had been considered at the time one of the Seven Wonders of the Ancient World. The Jewish historian Josephus describes this lighthouse in his work *The Jewish War*, in which he tells the history of the Jewish people from the beginning up through the first century AD.

Judaism—as explained by historians like Josephus, scholars of the Jewish faith, and rabbis—in all its celebrations and traditions offers a distinct and important understanding of light and dark. In the book of Genesis are the words, "And God said, 'Let there be light,' and there was light. And God saw the light was good, and He separated the light from darkness. God called the light 'day,' and the darkness He called 'night.'" This story of Creation for me isn't about some ultimate being determining night and day, but something deeper and more fundamental about life.

As you will note, God didn't do away with darkness. Darkness is a significant part of our world, as is light. And without darkness, we would never know light, or appreciate light. It is in the darkest nights that we can appreciate and see the brightest stars. It is in shadows that we can see the variations of light. And it is in understanding the darkness or the shadows of our hearts and souls that we can find our way to light and goodness.

The 16th century Spanish saint and mystic, John of the Cross, expressed this from his perspective when he wrote, "In the dark night of the soul, bright flows the river of God." St. John, who was mentored and befriended by the saint and mystic Teresa of Avila, served and suffered, experienced light and darkness in profound ways, and wrote a lengthy poem entitled "Dark Night of the Soul." Detroit native, former monk and psychotherapist Thomas Moore used the poem as a basis for his book *Dark Nights of the Soul* in which he wrote, "It is precisely because we resist the darkness in ourselves that we miss the depths of the loveliness, beauty, brilliance, creativity, and joy that lie at our core."

Scientists, cosmologists and astrophysicists also weigh in on the relationship between light and darkness in our universe, as they seek to understand what composes the light and what composes the dark. And we have come to understand from their studies, nearly all of the dark elements are actually composed of matter. Darkness is not nothingness. As the astrophysicist Neil deGrasse Tyson explains, "We're not inventing dark matter out of thin space; instead, we deduce its existence from observational facts. Dark matter is just as real as the many exoplanets discovered in orbit around stars other than the Sun, discovered solely through their gravitational influence on their host stars and not from direct measurement of their light."

Tyson, a child who attended public school in the Bronx, raised in a mixed-race family, grew up always stretching his curiosity to the stars. He was extremely curious to understand light and dark, and was inspired to explore the universe and all its mysteries even further by the light shown to him by another, astrophysicist and poet Carl Sagan. Sagan understood how the light and dark in each of us gives us a path to understanding the light and dark in the universe, as his own words highlight: "We are a way for the cosmos to know itself."

Ignoring our own shadows and individual darkness sets us on a path of not taking responsibility and accountability for wrong decisions and negative impacts we can have on the close circles in our lives and on the farther circles of the world. I hate to break it to you, but none of us is perfect. No great spiritual or political leader in the history of civilization has been perfect. Each, no matter how praiseworthy, has had shadows and darkness within. The more enlightened those leaders were, the more they understood the existence of light and dark in their own hearts. Just as darkness is not nothingness, it's also not evil; it just *is*.

It is often difficult, however, to examine and come to terms with our own darkness. We each like to convey to the outside world, and even in our own mirrors, that we are good, loving and nonjudgmental, and that it is only others who are filled with hate, prejudices and biases. In fact, we all have the shadows of hate and prejudices within our hearts whether we are aware of those or blissfully unaware. As Carl Jung, the Swiss psychiatrist, states, "People will do anything, no matter how absurd, in order to avoid facing their own souls. One does not become enlightened by imagining figures of light, but by making the darkness conscious."

Your skin color, the religions you were raised in or the lack thereof, where you grew up, your sex or sexual orientation, your education, your work experience, or any part of your life story has the great potential to embed biases. All of these inclinations and biases influence and direct how we think, talk or act as we relate to the world. The journey to a more evolved way of being in the world is through self-reflection, recognizing our own shadows and striving to overcome our inherent biases. Our task is in self-revelation and probing within deeply as we uncover our darkness. When we open ourselves to that revelation, we are then more free to choose to pursue and follow the light.

We must ask ourselves some really tough questions in this regard so that we can explore and unearth our shadows. We might not even know initially what this darkness is or how rooted it is in at least part of determining decisions we make and judgments we have. It is through this process of reflection and self-accountability that we can identify the light as well, and allow that light to shine ever brighter in dark spaces. The point is not to do away with the darkness, but to acknowledge it.

As you read in a previous chapter, I highlighted a quote from the writer Anne Morrow Lindbergh who moved through her own waves of light and dark. She was famously married to world-wide hero and pioneer aviator Charles Lindbergh, so she had to navigate having a relationship with a public figure and all that entailed. Whereas many of us have the advantage of some privacy, her life played out publicly while she struggled through emotional abuse from her husband. This emotional turmoil included her discovery that her husband had a whole other family and life that she was unaware of for most of her marriage. And she experienced one of the most tragic events in life, the kidnapping and murder of her oldest child, which also played out for the entire world to see, know and speculate about.

We too frequently look out at the world and label someone as worse than us, so we can feel better about our own darkness. Yes, there are some really bad people in the world—dreadful individuals who have no moral compass and who only seem to cast dark shadows over others. Absolutely, we are each called from our moral center to confront hatred and injustice as strongly and fiercely as we can. However, if we really want to move our lives toward a more loving and compassionate space, we need to first face our own shadows and darkness. Yes, there are main actors and superstars in the play of dark and light, but we are also supporting players in the drama.

A long while back, I had a big professional decision to make in my life that I knew was a key point in determining how I would move forward. My professional career was, in my heart, not fulfilling and lacked meaning, and that situation was impacting my personal life by making me less compassionate and present, and more impatient and angry. I intuitively decided that a visit to a lighthouse would help me to evaluate my life and make some decisions at this turning point.

I discovered, in the search for the right lighthouse to help me find my way, that I could actually stay overnight at the Big Bay Lighthouse on the shores of Lake Superior near Marquette, Michigan. I drove there across the solitary roads of Michigan, not fully understanding exactly why, and stayed a few days. I was able to determine the way forward in my moments in that lighthouse. I sat and read, felt and thought, and the decision became obvious. I needed to leave the company I had founded and built, and to chart a new course. Immediately following this determination, I had a sense of relief and calm. I knew there would be struggles ahead, and much was unknown, but I knew the change I was going to make was crucial.

Lighthouses are such a fascinating structure to me and a good bit of a paradox as well. They stand all in the darkness, "accepting" it, but they provide light when it is needed. In the shadows of the shore, lighthouses are both welcoming, and they are a warning. They welcome wayward ships or passersby to come to a safe harbor in the midst of storms and troubled waters, or to come rest in the midst of a long journey. The lighthouses are also a warning of dangerous rocks or a shore-line that could do damage when the light is low and darkness covers the way.

Lighthouses are also designed to provide an intermittent beacon and horn to signal to others about their existence: messaging the welcoming or warning they were built to convey. Interestingly, they don't provide a constant light or a constant sound. In between the signals of light and sound are spaces of dark and quiet. And it is those spaces of darkness that allow their light to do their work. A lighthouse wouldn't be a lighthouse if not for the presence of darkness.

And so, too, it is important we understand our own selves as lighthouses of a kind. Do we want to be a place of safety and welcoming to our fellow travelers? Do we want to give warnings to those we love about potential dangers in life? Do we want to provide rest or warmth to those in need? If so, it is important we understand the need to sit more comfortably in our darkness—rather than denying or fearing it, and use our dark sides in a way that makes our light brighter and more useful for others.

The lighthouse of our life may be in a bit of disrepair, or need greater caretaking. If so, let us each take the time to do some remodeling and sprucing up, but in the meantime, we can still provide light and words of comfort to others. Though more importantly, in those times of needed improvements, let us give light and comfort to our own hearts and souls. And if we understand and accept our dark spaces and shadow selves, it will give us a greater capacity for the same in fellow travelers.

Our own lighthouse may seem beautiful or perfect to others because they are only looking at mere appearances. However, our light could be low, or maybe our signaling is malfunctioning, preventing us from shining in the night and darkness when we are most needed. Can we be a lighthouse in the dark, to others and ourselves, as much as we are in the brightness of the day? My hope is that whatever our condition happens to be, we all strive to do the work required to be the best lighthouse we can be in this moment, on this day.

We look out at the world, and it can be a dark place. It is filled with shadows, and we sometimes struggle to see any light. We search for the sunrise in the deepest part of night, and we worry and wait anxiously for light, sometimes even shouting into the darkness. We so desperately want a lighthouse to appear to guide us and humanity through the difficulties and disruptions. Maybe the lighthouse we are really looking for is on our shore, and in our own homes.

In order to navigate the often times dangerous Great Lakes in the nights of cold, stiff winds and darkness, one lighthouse isn't all that helpful. A single lighthouse will only take us a very short distance, and get us out of the danger only just directly in front of us. There are hundreds of lighthouses throughout each lake that together provide the path forward. Each one necessary to accomplish the overall task, each one giving way to the next so that we can get to our destination.

And the same is true for navigating life and this world. One lighthouse won't do the trick, one new job won't fundamentally change our lives, and one political leader won't solve all our problems. We each can be a lighthouse, together with others, to make the path clearer and safer to get us through the journey of this life, and bring our communities to safety.

Whenever we as a country or community face crisis or are in dark times, a string of lights of compassionate people shine. People put their own needs aside in the moment to lend a hand. We see this in the aftermath of hurricanes or earthquakes or forest fires. We have seen this and still see it in the folks who stepped up as we all suffered through a pandemic. And I saw this in Texas as millions lost power and water, and couldn't find food or warmth; others arose to solve the problem or fill a need. Even when our political leaders dropped the ball, weren't available or lacked empathy, average Americans stepped forward and became lighthouses.

Maybe by looking at our shadows and darkness and thence revealing our own light, it can give us empathy and motivation for the humanness of our fellow man and woman. By finding our purpose in some way in life as a lighthouse to others, we can discover meaning and joy in the part we play in service. And then, as I experienced in Big Bay, a sense of peace and calm can settle in, and we can be an important player in a new creation story—of our life and the life of our country.

Lighthouse

Built on a shore
Solid in structure
Guiding to safety
Into a harbor
Warning of danger
Of rocks and shoals
A light repeats
In rhythmic beauty
A horn blares
Better beware
A keeper minds
The signals daily
For friend or foe
Neighbor or stranger
A mission of care
In the middle of nowhere
Walking the steps
To keep a light aflame
For community and country
In a land of patriots
We all can be
A keeper of light

7
Forgiveness and Reconciliation

"True reconciliation is never cheap, for it is based on forgiveness which is costly. Forgiveness in turn depends on repentance, which has to be based on an acknowledgment of what was done wrong, and therefore on disclosure of the truth. You cannot forgive what you do not know."

These words of South African Anglican cleric and theologian Desmund Tutu were in reference to a country as it struggled to reconcile and forgive in the midst of trauma and struggle, but they apply to each of us as individuals and in the relationships we have at the most basic level. He chaired the Truth and Reconciliation Commission in South Africa in the aftermath of apartheid to put in place restorative justice. Tutu helped teach and unite a country through memories of hate and discrimination; he also can speak to our hearts and souls no matter where we live.

We are often told by our parents, teachers or other advice-giving people to forgive and forget. The advice is to move on after someone betrays our trust or hurts us and to get over it so that we can live our lives more at peace. While there is some truth in these exhortations, these simple words of wisdom also bely a deeper and more complex truth that often is in conflict with how we will find a place of peace and uncover and restore justice.

The question becomes: how do we resolve the equally important values of truth and accountability in conjunction with forgiveness? How can we live a life of more peace and see justice established while simultaneously letting go of the load we carry of the poison within our own souls when we can't forgive? We want to see those responsible held accountable for their actions. Waves of anger fill us as we see damage caused by perpetrators, either to us or to other individuals or to society as a whole. And we know that at some point, while the anger can and should move us to action to better establish justice, we must find a way to forgive and reconcile so we don't stay stuck in rage. We want the perpetrators punished, but we know deep down the punishment itself won't give us peace.

One of the major impediments to reconciliation is that our society, religions, culture, legal system and our personal interactions are based primarily on the idea of punitive justice, where the main goal is to punish. If we approached our interactions through the prism of restorative justice where the goal is to underscore responsibility, while seeking to reconcile, repair and move ahead more holistically, then reconciliation becomes much more likely and available to us. Fania E. Davis, civil rights attorney and founding director of Restorative Justice for Oakland Youth, explains that restorative justice is, "[a] justice that seeks not to punish, but to heal. A justice that seeks to transform broken lives, relationships, and communities, rather than shatter them further. A justice that seeks reconciliation, rather than a deepening of conflict." But this process is complicated and requires many steps and a lot of effort to achieve, and skipping certain steps will derail the endeavor.

In the last year in our country, there have been demands for reconciliation and unity as we all observe the hurt others are suffering, the damage done to our democratic institutions, and damage done to our reputation domestically and internationally. In fact, Joe Biden ran an entire campaign based on the idea of unity and healing our nation from the terrible divides and division that do such incredible harm to who we really are. In the aftermath of Congress certifying the Electoral College results, he spoke the words, "Now it is time to turn the page, to unite, to heal."

Biden's message is and was laudable, but the reality of life and politics is a bit more complicated than that campaign slogan. I believe Biden knows this (he has lived a life in the rough and tumble of politics) and was calling us, as Lincoln did 150 years ago, to our better angels. In fact, President Biden—in his first few months in office—has struggled to bring about this conversion from division to unity. The question remains, what are the steps we need to take to get to unity and reconciliation, and should we really ever forget and forgive? This is a question not only for our country, but just as importantly, for how we act in our daily life when we are subjected to hurt or have been treated wrongly.

The second impeachment trial of former President Donald Trump held in the winter of 2021 gives us some insights into how we might bring together these seemingly disparate values of responsibility and reconciliation. True, former President Trump did not receive the final punishment of getting convicted in the Senate, and that was an unfortunate miscarriage of justice. However, the punishment, in my view, was the least important aspect of what unfolded in the Senate in the arguments over whether Trump should be convicted. If your goal was exclusively punitive justice and not restorative, then you might feel the trial was a failure.

Before we get to reconciliation as a country and heal our wounds, the first step in the process is finding out what the truth is about what has occurred and determining who is accountable for the damage, considering not just the accountability of one person, but for others who might have enabled or facilitated the problem, and for society as a whole, which created the fertile ground for injustice to sprout up. In restoration, we must explore both individual responsibility as well as what in our culture and communication helped breed the actions.

I know many were disappointed with the final outcome of this impeachment trial related to the tragic events of January 6th where thousands of armed people stormed the U.S. Capitol and did damage to property and human life. But through the course of the lengthy hours of testimony, we did get to some truths, and accountability was revealed. The most important goal was to raise awareness of what happened, and who was responsible in many different ways for the damage to our country. And in that way, the trial was a success.

The successful history of South Africa in moving from the stain of apartheid to a more open and just democracy showed that reconciliation happened because truth was put first, and only in its aftermath could reconciliation occur. Nelson Mandela, the first President of a modern South Africa, said in 1995, "Reconciliation does not mean forgetting or trying to bury the pain of conflict, but that reconciliation means working together to correct the legacy of past injustice." I don't know if the new post-apartheid leadership in South Africa took lessons from our own American history in our missteps and mistakes, but Mandela, Tutu and other South African leaders did a much better job of correcting injustice than we did as a country more than a century ago.

The last time we as a nation faced a group of people who attempted to disrupt the peaceful transfer of power and wanted to nullify an election was 1860. We fought a bloody and destructive Civil War where hundreds of thousands of our fellow men and women perished. And President Lincoln's vision of the perfecting of our union through a process of Reconstruction never came to fruition in large part because he was assassinated as the war came to a close. And our country paid the price for decades following.

In his second Inaugural address, Lincoln called us to reconciliation: "With malice toward none, with charity for all, with firmness in the right as God gives us to see the right, let us strive on to finish the work we are in; to bind up the nation's wounds; to care for him who shall have borne the battle, and for his widow and his orphan—to do all which may achieve and cherish a just and lasting peace, among ourselves, and with all nations." Lincoln also understood inherently that we must go through the process of accountability and reconstruction before we could authentically get to that healing.

After Lincoln's death, the path chosen by the next President was an attempt at unity without following the first steps of revealing truth and assessing accountability, and it then took over a hundred years before we passed the Civil Rights and

Voting Rights Acts with an expansion of democracy and justice that we fought a civil war to achieve. Because of the lack of accountability, America saw a rise of the same injustice and discrimination that led us to civil war. While slavery was outlawed, Americans experienced the establishment of Jim Crow laws to keep black Americans from voting, thousands of lynchings of our innocent citizens, the deaths of way too many civil rights leaders, and inequitable laws and an unjust economic system.

And we are still in the midst of this despicable situation today with the rise of white supremacy, the callous mistreatment of people of color, and discrimination based on race, religion and ethnicity. In fact, many of the mob at the Capitol on January 6th were carrying the Confederate flag as if the Civil War was still going on. One of the main revelations of the trial in the Senate and what we have observed over the last few years is that the self-evident truth that all men and women are created equal is still unaccepted by a portion of our country.

In fact, the newest Attorney General Merrick Garland, who prosecuted the terrorists Timothy McVeigh and Terry Nichols, responsible for the bombing of the Alfred P. Murrah federal building in Oklahoma City in 1995, raised just this point in his confirmation hearings before the Senate Judiciary Committee in February. Garland emphasized that "there's a line from Oklahoma City, and there's another line all the way back to the experiences I mentioned in my opening, with respect to the battles of the original Justice Department against the Ku Klux Klan. We are facing a more dangerous period than we faced in Oklahoma City and at that time."

Justice and reconciliation, as Garland suggested, come from understanding the linkage between events, and then systematically undertaking a level of deep reformation. Just as change in our own life comes in a step-by-step process, the same is true for our country. And even though we might lose an individual battle, increasing awareness, discovering the truth, and determining accountability allows us to grow and evolve to a more enlightened place. The history of the success of the civil rights movement has valuable lessons for each of us in the way we must keep moving, and continue to seek further and deeper success.

In 1955, the young black man Emmett Till was unjustly killed by two racist white men in Mississippi. A trial was held in Sumner, Mississippi, where clear and convincing evidence was presented to an all-white jury of the guilt of these two men. And in the course of the trial, the country's segregation, injustice and unfairness were fully on display. It only took 68 minutes for this jury to come back with a not guilty verdict for the two white men who killed Till.

Yes, in this particular battle, the forces of justice lost in the punishment phase of the trial, but the civil rights movement took this loss and turned it into success because of the way injustice was highlighted for all to see. Those involved knew inherently punishment is not the primary goal in moral society. Not long after this verdict in the Till trial, seamstress and civil rights activist Rosa Parks was arrested on a bus in Montgomery, Alabama, and the bus boycott began in earnest. This then led to the sit-ins at lunch counters around the country, and ultimately to the freedom march over the Edmund Pettus bridge from Selma to Montgomery. And within ten years of Till's death, President Lyndon Johnson signed the historic Civil and Voting Rights Acts.

Yes, there were many tragic points along the way in the path to justice, and many battles lost. But at each setback, the civil rights movement grew in strength; pursued truth, justice and accountability; and ultimately achieved steps in the advancement and restoration of justice. In so many instances in the world and American history, we can recognize both the loss in a particular battle and the gain and ultimate success because of perseverance and the revealing of truth.

I am not writing here for a history lesson, or to convince you of some particular political persuasion, or to tell you that all will be fine. I use these examples of our current history and other historical unfolding movements to shine a light on our own journey to healing, reconciliation and forgiveness. We look at history not only as an examination of society or civilization change, but for lessons about our own individual change and reformation.

Should we forget what happened in our own life when another has hurt us or done damage to a relationship? No, and it is probably impossible anyway to completely erase a wound. We carry with us until our last breath the pains we've endured…just as in our country's history, we should never forget when America has fallen down and failed, because it is in the not forgetting where we learn lessons for moving forward.

But in not forgetting, that doesn't mean we can't forgive. Ultimately, we forgive not as a benefit to the other, but as a way for us to reconcile our own conflicts within our hearts. We forgive as a gift to ourselves. However, just because we forgive doesn't mean we welcome back in the same way with open arms someone that betrayed our trust.

If a friend of mine who I welcome into my house, to guard over my possessions and my children, steals from me and hurts my children, it doesn't mean just because I forgive them, they once again get to babysit my kids or be trusted by me going forward in the same way. I can forgive, but I also can learn a lesson from the history of this relationship. Can I be reconciled with this person in the path of forgiveness; can the relationship be restored in some new way, and can trust possibly be rebuilt? Sure, but it takes time.

In our personal relationships, as well as in healing our country and overcoming divides, it requires some definitive steps in the process of forgiveness to get to reconciliation. It requires truth and accountability. Just as in the recent impeachment trial, individuals in intimate relationships, seeking to forgive, must hold up truth and accountability in order heal wounds and grow.

What must occur in my life long before I get to reconciliation? I must see responsibility taken by the person who harmed or hurt me and an admission of truth by the offender. I must sense some authentic remorse in the person for what they have done and an understanding of the damage their words or actions caused—not a throwaway, "I'm sorry," carrying little emotional attachment, but a heartfelt expression of regret.

After some conveyance of responsibility and remorse, I think to get to reconciliation there also needs to be repair and then reform. The person or persons who committed the wrongful act will need to repair any damage caused by the hurt. If one is truly sorry, they would sincerely want to fix what they broke, to clean up any mess they caused, and at the very least leave the "home" as they originally found it, if not in better condition than before.

And finally, in this process, we must understand and clearly know that the offender has reformed their actions going forward in ways we can trust. We must be assured they have fundamentally changed their approach and way they think, talk and act. This almost always requires some amount of soul searching and introspection, involving a lot of time and work. It is not a microwave meal ready in 60 seconds or sprint of 60 yards. It is a marathon of many miles proved out in a lengthy process.

And even with all these demonstrations, how we get back to trust and reconciliation is going to involve slow movements and can't be quickly demanded. It isn't acceptable for the person who did the wrong to say to us, "See, I did all the following and now you must forgive me and reconcile with me and welcome me back in the fold." The offending party can't act as if it is now our responsibility to avoid the breakdown in the relationship. If someone does this, it probably is a fairly good sign they haven't genuinely gone through the responsibility steps in a meaningful way.

Our country—and many disadvantaged, non-privileged groups—have been hurt in our nation's history, and this is particularly true over the last few years. To repair the damage done in the 2020 election cycle, the process of reconciliation will need to unfold in very similar ways as illustrated above. The damagers, which includes many voters who facilitated the events, will need to acknowledge truth, take responsibility, express remorse, assist in repairing damage, and reform their behaviors. And until that occurs, reconciliation is a pipe dream. Same as it would be in our personal relationships.

We each have the choice of how we accept people back into our trust, and the timing and ways are always very personal. We often make mistakes in accepting people back in too quickly, or we delay it for too long. We must find the balance in the art of reconciliation and forgiveness. For me, I have learned over many years that as I continue to hold an intention of rec- onciliation, I allow myself the space and time to see and feel clearly. When I do get to a place where I can make a decision to forgive, it is authentic and not just based on a desire for things to get back to normal or have some artificial restoration of the relationship.

Yes, let us forgive, though forgetting is probably something we should just forget about. Let us instead remember and recall events in our own life and circumstances in our nation's history that inform us in ways that help us bring peace to ourselves and others. And let us also know that losing a battle on one day or moment doesn't mean we didn't achieve steps toward truth and responsibility as we struggled and suffered. So, forgive yourself if you are still learning all those lessons; I know I do each day.

A New Truth

A pecan limb falls
Crashing loudly
On a metal roof
Shielding a home
Damage is done
Peace is shattered
Rolling off awkwardly
Upon Earth's dirt floor

Lies quietly in humility
Waiting to be found
Repairs are made
Dents cleaned up
The limb never says sorry
Knowing it is
Up to the other only
Make use of me it pines
It is broken in pieces
Used for a fire
To warm and to light
Its new purpose and meaning
Its new truth
And once again
The two have found unity

8
Concentric Circles of Life

"Midway along the journey of our life, I woke to find myself in a dark wood,
for I had wandered off from the straight path."

The Italian philosopher and poet Dante Alighieri wrote these
words in the Middle Ages, at a time of great unrest, conflict and
disruption, not completely unlike our own today. In his seminal
work *The Divine Comedy*, Dante describes his journey into the
circles of Hell, Heaven and Purgatory, led either by the ancient
Roman poet Virgil or by his "ideal woman" Beatrice. Though it
was an imaginary journey into the afterlife, Dante's writing was
applicable and instructive for how our soul perceives good and
evil and how we might live in real life. So, what does an Italian
poet born in the 13th century have to teach us about living life
in the 21st century?

In a life from years ago, I advised companies, candidates
and foundations in how to communicate with key audiences in
order to get their messages through with the hope of winning
customers, votes, and policy objectives. The audiences could
be a small group of key influential people or the news media,

or they could stretch all the way out to the large general public. And while we can maintain consistency and integrity in the core of what we want to say, how we communicate to each can be quite different. There may be fundamentally different ways that messages are received depending upon the audience and the levels of trust that must be established and maintained.

In this process of creating strategies for each of these entities, a revelation came to me of a concentric circle communications model, based in a vague way on Dante's writing. One could design a concentric circle approach based on how operations in business or politics communicate outwardly and how communications might be received inwardly—not a circle of hell, or heaven or purgatory like Dante, though some meetings I have been in felt like hell or purgatory. In this model, the smaller inner circle might contain the most influential and key audiences, working out concentrically to larger and larger circles of folks we need to communicate with to accomplish our shared goal.

An example from politics may help illustrate this a bit more succinctly. As a strategist who helped George W. Bush run for President, let me explain. In the innermost circle of the campaign effort might be the candidate and his or her family, key advisors and friends. This inner circle is where the bond is greatest, where the belief and trust in each other is deepest, and where discussion is most extensive and, in many ways, most intimate.

As a presidential campaign works its way out from this most tight inner circle, you then hit the circle of those closest to and supportive of the candidate. This circle contains the smaller number of people who one can lean on and who are likely, after the innermost circle, the most supportive and can be some of the greatest advocates. This might include key political party officials or funders of the campaign, elected officials who have loyal allegiance to the candidate, or a loyal supporter who has a wider circle of contacts they can influence.

The third concentric circle would be a much broader group of supporters or contributors who want to help the campaign. Both supporters and contributors have a desire and ability to communicate with voters in different ways through actual direct conversation or symbolic action based on their influence in the community. There is some level of trust in this circle among the candidate, supporters and contributors, but not at the level of the closer circles to the campaign and the candidate.

A fourth circle might be the news media, which has a broad reach to the large pool of voters who decide the election. Reporters, news anchors and journalists, who in many ways are the prism by which voters hear what the campaign is saying, are often the interpreters for the general public concerning the communications of the campaign effort. In most presidential campaigns, the only way to reach a large segment of voters in an authentic way is through the medium of this circle of the press. Though in today's "news" environment of cable and the internet, the line has been rather fuzzy between who the journalists are and who the advocates are, complicating which circle they really fall into.

And finally, after going through possible other, ever broader circles of key advocates in a neighborhood or community, one reaches the extensive and vast group of the millions of voters that a candidate and campaign need to ultimately convince and build trust accordingly. This is the circle that must be won over if the candidate is going to win the election, build support for a mandate around a vision, and accomplish the political agenda that is being pursued. And it is to target this circle that most campaigns try to come up with some slogan to communicate what captures, in a broad way, their rationale for running, as President Obama did with a simple word of "Hope," and President Trump did with "Make America Great Again."

In this concentric circle model of communication, whether it be for a candidate or a company, communication isn't only one way and doesn't necessarily have to go through each separate circle to reach all of the groups or audiences. A campaign can utilize each circle to communicate to the adjacent circle, relying on a smaller group to engage with the larger adjacent group, all the way out to the final audience. Or, for example, the campaign can jump directly from the innermost circle all the way out to the broader circle with advertising on television, radio or the internet, or some form of direct voter contact like mail (actual or virtual), phone calls or canvassing from home to home. Keep in mind as one skips over circles, the authenticity of the message is diminished because trust hasn't been established directly by the candidate or original source of the message.

The most effective campaigns understand that communication is a two-way street; it goes in directions both outward from the most closely gathered group to the farthest away, and it goes inward from the public all the way back to the ultimate smallest circle. We communicate to the influentials, the press and the public, and we must also be open and allow communications to come from those outer circles back in. This allows for understanding audiences more, for building relationships in a more trusting way, and for revising tactics and strategies to be more effective. The best campaigns understand that in politics or in selling a product for a business it is about not only telling folks what you want to say, but about listening and understanding what voters or consumers want to hear. These successful campaigns are disciplined on both strategy and messaging, and they are also fluid, allowing for evolution as the political or consumer environment demands.

As I have walked, and like Dante "wandered off from the straight path," on my land along the Blanco River amidst the Cypress and Live Oak trees, I have realized one can approach one's life in a similar manner. We can consider how these concentric circles are utilized in a professional or political way. And we can examine our own worlds and how we might understand the various groupings we interact with in different ways. Nature, too, has concentric circles of interaction and interplay.

The hawks that fly over my home and nest in the trees practice their own version of concentric circles. They keep a nest in which only their closest offspring and bonded mates can feel safe and protected. The adult males and females venture out to carefully build this nest from twigs and other bits and pieces of nature. They utilize parts outside their circle to support their nest and provide comfort, sending a message that they can be trusted and will provide security.

As these hawks fly over the natural surroundings looking for food for offspring, they dive into the river to collect a fish swimming in its own circle. They bring back this food to nourish their eyas. The adult hawks warn others not to come too close, but they know innately that even the most dangerous parts of the broader circles are all part of their natural world. And when it is time, the baby offspring are pushed out of the nest, to an outer circle, so they can create their own life and their new inner circles. The mother and father hawks don't love them less, just differently.

From politics, products, hawks or even the beehives here nestled close to the hills on my land, we all experience an existence of concentric circles. Like the circles we may design a campaign structure around or those that we observe in nature, we could consider our own circles involved in our daily existence in a similar way. As Rafiki counseled to Simba in the movie and play *The Lion King*, "It's the Circle of Life and it moves us all, through despair and hope, through faith and love, 'til we find our place on the path unwinding. In the Circle. The Circle of Life."

Each of us desires to have trust and communication in all aspects of our lives. We want to communicate and build relationships with those closest to us and to those far out in the distant circle of people we might never meet, but whom we want to impact in some positive way. We each are individuals, but we are born into a world where connection and cooperation and communication are a necessity. We want to be genuinely understood, for our messages not to get lost in translation.

How we communicate and relate to our most intimate circle is and should be very different than how we communicate and relate to other circles of folks in our life. We also must first consider who we even welcome into the innermost circle. Those people will know us in the most intimate ways. Of course it makes sense that we will communicate differently with them than others we come across on our paths.

We often want to define ourselves as trustworthy, trusting, open and loyal. However, do we have to have the same level of trust, openness and loyalty within every concentric circle of our relationships and networks? The answer I believe is no. We can be a loyal or trusting person, but also decide at what level of trust or loyalty different people fall in the circles of our lives. And the way we communicate with each of those circles can and should be fundamentally different.

As I stood under a Cypress tree that grew tall, solid and rooted, I reflected on who exactly is in my innermost circle and who are others that are farther out on the rings of my world. Inside my most intimate circle, as a person of faith, I knew that God was there. Though at times of struggle, like other intimates, He/She frustrated me and I wondered where God had gone, I could always come back to that connection. I knew and know that my connection with God was one of the most trusting relationships I had.

Also in that intimate circle, I welcome those I love most dearly and openly. This circle included my children when they were young, but as they have grown up and established their own lives and deep connections away from family, my children have moved out to a circle just adjacent to this closest one to me. My adult kids are absolutely essential to me, but as they left home and went out into the world, I have realized each of our levels of openness with each other would adjust. What they share in their most intimate relations doesn't have to be shared with me, and vice-versa.

When we get divorced or end a relationship, we don't keep those partners in the same circle that they might have been in at one point in our lives. Our levels of openness, loyalty and trust will change depending upon where a person is now in our life, not locked into where they might have been at some point.

Does this mean we aren't still loyal and open with folks who have moved circles? No. We just have to adapt the level of communication and intimacy to match the new reality.

As people move in and out of our various concentric circles, it is imperative that we adjust our own expectations and push back against any inappropriate expectations of how loyal, how open and how trusting we need to be. It doesn't mean we don't care about them, or aren't still close to them, or want what is best for them. It just means they reside in a different place in our life now.

This movement of people in and out of the circles of our worlds can be difficult, wrenching and upsetting at times. And we must give ourselves and others patience in the processing of where they sit in the concentric ripples of our own path. We also realize along the way that we may have welcomed people into a circle where they didn't belong, or we shut out someone from a circle where they should have been. As with campaigns, this needs to be an organic process, where we learn from our missteps, or we grow in the capacity to more readily determine who falls into what category. Just because we welcomed someone into a circle they didn't belong in, it doesn't mean we have to keep them there out of some false sense of loyalty.

For example, some of us make the mistake of thinking that because we have shared physical intimacy with another that they belong in the most intimate circle. While I think the ideal would be that integration of closeness and sexuality, it often doesn't work out that way. This is true of the opposite as well, where we think because we share a level of connection with another, we jump to considering physical closeness with that person when this might not be the healthiest path.

We might have siblings (I have 10 of them, nine living) or close friends who we (or they) think should all be in the same circle. While it might be a nice idea for that to be the case, the level of trust and openness is going to be different depending upon our bonds and extent of the depth of connection. Again, this might cause disturbances in our relationships or frustrations in others, but keeping someone where they don't belong—or allowing others to make assumptions about where they think they belong because we haven't been clear—in the long term will only cause more hurt, pain or misunderstanding.

As we look out into the larger concentric circles of our life, as a campaign would, we can offer a consistent level of love and caring to all, but how that is practiced will be fundamentally different. Each of us, if we are mission or purpose driven, and if we desire to have an impact on the world larger than just in our homes, will want to reach a larger audience in our communications. This mission might be our vision of the world we want to see and possibly live in. If we believe in that mission, we will seek to extend our reach of caring and concern to the farthest circle we can.

And in that way, it will become a two-way conversation. We will express our core principles and goals in words and actions, and we hope it will be received and land in a meaningful and impactful way. We also will need to listen to those others in the circles of our life and adapt what we are doing. At times we will need to change the manner in which we communicate and care so that the possibility of success rises. If our goal is to bring positive change to people's lives and the world, why wouldn't we adjust to those outer circles so that what we are doing has more impact?

As we move outward in the campaign of our life, we must be careful not to forget our core and who lands where in our world. If we don't have definitive principles as well as boundaries, we can easily get lost and trip up. Sometimes we grow tired or feel under attack; we lose strength to communicate clearly, and our discipline or motivation wanes. We have people in our life who push and prod us to offer a deeper level of openness and trust than what that person really has earned. In those times, it is likely best to go back to the closest circle to us and take a break. It is what candidates do when they become exhausted on the campaign trail or when they need renewed focus. Jesus even did the same at times when he went off alone or with a couple of disciples to pray and regather himself so he could more effectively be in the world and share his message.

If you are on social media too much, and find yourself overwhelmed or confused, anxious or angry, take a break. Social media has a way of confusing circles. If your friends or family are pushing too much, retreat a bit and rest in the sanctuary of your most intimate circle. If you are a person of faith, connect again with the God you believe in. If you are not a religious person, find that place in nature or in those things that bring you peace and your heart comfort.

Some may read this discussion, and think there is no way you can live with what you may perceive as maintaining superficial relationships in this concentric circle approach. I understand that, and it took me many years to come to a place where I can establish these levels of distinctions of people in my life. I am still learning and continue to do it imperfectly. If it resonates and makes sense to you, maybe it will help in coming to an understanding where others belong in your life, or where you fit in a certain relationship...what circle of someone else's life you are in. If it's not quite resonating, then explore your own version of working through how you determine who fits where in your world and what level of communication is most effective and authentic with each person or group.

Every campaign I have ever worked on has been different, and I learned something new and adapted. And every relationship in life has brought me to where I am today through steps forward, steps back, loss and learning. As I explore the concentric circles surrounding me, I know that I will find myself at times in a "dark wood." And I also know the light of my closest connections will lead me through.

An Older Sister

Number one
Of an Irish tribe
An enormous heart
A beautiful mind
A healing hand
For children
And all families
Wicked smart
Wonderful soul
Leading in life
As she serves each day
She finds her way
Through mountains
And valleys
Not an easy life

She has an ease
Walking in nature
She feels at peace
Connected to this Earth
She sleeps
Under the stars
I hope she knows
The light she is
How others she has touched
Including a brother
In this Celtic circle

9
Legacies

"Everyone must leave something behind when he dies, my grandfather said. A child or a book or a painting or a house or a wall built or a pair of shoes made... It doesn't matter what you do, he said, so long as you change something from the way it was before you touched it into something that's like you after you take your hands away."

When the writer Ray Bradbury wrote these words in his widely acclaimed futuristic novel *Fahrenheit 451*, published in 1953, he was very concerned, worried and anxious about the world in which he was living and what would become of society ahead. While writing this impactful work, he had just come out of and struggled through the horrific events of World War II. Bradbury was appalled at the book burning of Adolph Hitler's Nazi regime and the repression by Soviet autocrat Joseph Stalin.

Bradbury started writing around the age of 11 in the midst of the Great Depression, and sometimes the only paper he could jot his words down on was butcher paper. His family had little money, and he could not afford college, so Bradbury went to the public library and became basically self-educated. Bradbury, in his life's accomplishments, definitely left something behind, as all of us have a dream of doing.

We frequently have heroes in our lives that extend back into a distant past, whether it be writers, fighters for justice and equality, spiritual leaders, or artists who had a significant impact, and we repeat their words and reference their works today. We longingly reflect back on them and dream of a better world in general or feel inspired to envision improvements we can directly make in our personal worlds. Yes, we have heroes in our present, but the past ones will always call to us, often with more fervor as we marvel at how much purpose and meaning their lives had.

We consider our heroes, but then move on—distinguishing them as extraordinary people and raising them up on a pedestal far removed from our routines—and we go about what we believe our ordinary lives to be. We do our schoolwork. We work in our jobs. We run errands. Or we plod through the daily home tasks of cleaning, cooking and doing laundry. It is as if these people we read about in history books are over there, and we are here, and there is a grand gulf separating us.

A quiet voice within our hearts sometimes calls us to something more. How should I be living out my existence now? Or our soul asks, what are you doing in this world to have an impact? This voice is often attached to some of those messages we encountered in our heroes of the past. We can either listen to this call within, or we can fill our days with even more of what we consider mundane tasks, and keep doing what we're already doing.

We hold up those figures in history books, touting their values as crucial in our society. Sometimes we use them as arrows to point to what we see as missing pieces in our leaders at this moment. We point a finger, and say, why aren't there Lincolns in power, or where are the Martin Luther Kings, or how come we don't have more Amelia Earharts. We wonder why others' values aren't aligned with our heroes, and even at times demand change in our current leaders based on our understanding of historical figures.

Do we pause long enough to look at our own hearts and lives, and confront our own possible misalignment with those values we admire? Do we examine how we are fighting for justice, or ask ourselves if we have the courage to ascend to new heights, or what words and acts we can contribute as we walk on this planet? How are we honoring the legacy of those who have come before that we so readily quote?

The genuine way of honoring those who have changed the world before us isn't really about going to museums dedicated to their lives and legacies. It isn't in reading the latest biography that tells us about their lives, or celebrating their birthday or movement they represented. All those are important things to do in the path of understanding and receptiveness to lessons to be learned, and ideals to be highlighted. But we aren't honoring the legacy truly unless we are aligned with why we adore these heroes and then live accordingly.

We don't honor the good news of Jesus by going to church, or saying some set of daily prayer, or putting a cross or other religious symbol on our walls. Yes, those are all symbolic reminders of what Jesus stood for and died for, but the real question is how we are incorporating his message of love in our own life. And how might we be living out his words from the Sermon on the Mount.

Neither do we fully honor Dr. King, and all his work for equality and justice, by going to the churches he preached from, or rereading the "I Have a Dream" speech he gave at the Mall in Washington, D.C. In addition to all that, we should ask how we are taking steps toward his dream today. How are we practicing his strategy of nonviolence and antiracism, and embracing love…beyond throwing out one of his quotes on social media? In what ways is our life in or out of sync with our heroes we so readily worship?

If we allow these renowned leaders of our past to only be remembered in a quote on a card or a picture on our wall but forgotten in our hearts—if we fail to put their wisdom into practice in this actual moment—then are we really honoring their legacy? What did all the battles they fought—many lost—mean if we don't continue the fight for a better world in the present? If we don't attempt to live out those legacies, then the meaning of their efforts and dreams becomes diminished. Their existence can become limited to their images, and to stories we only tell on holidays.

The land I live on now, before I became its owner, had become completely overgrown and filled with debris through the natural occurrence of fallen trees and limbs, rock slides, and junk left as the river would rise and deposit what it carried, then retreat back to its banks. A few years before I had acquired the land, Mother Nature let loose, as she often does, to remind us we are not always in charge.

In 2015, there was a "five-hundred-year flood" event here where the Blanco River rose more that 40 feet over its normal levels. This historic flood wiped out homes and damaged property, resulting in some cases of serious injury and death. In the aftermath, many folks had to start the process of reconstruction and rebuilding. Some, unfortunately, had to abandon their original homes and start over completely. The slogan "Wimberley Strong" was strewn all over the small town, on flags flown in yards and businesses, and in words scrolled across buildings. And the property I ended up buying was one of those unfortunate places where the original home was wiped off the foundation. The owners had moved on to more secure surroundings, and the land was seriously scarred.

It took a good bit of time, for myself, some friends and a local family of men I hired, to clean it up and create the beautiful space I am blessed to live on. I could see the property in a vision—what it could look like and become, even in the midst of the shape it was currently in. And then, the work of the present, despite all the former obstacles and trauma, transformed it into the vision I had. I look fondly out my window and feel great satisfaction in what I was able to do with sacrifice, sweat and effort.

But I know if I don't maintain this land, and give it the necessary attention on a regular basis, it will begin to revert back to what is was before. It would become overgrown and filled with junk. So it is with life. I know that if I just sat back in my satisfaction with my property and left it alone for a year or so, it would be as if I never did the work to begin with. It would be like the beauty that I created and the work I did never had meaning.

When I was young growing up in Michigan, the third of us 11 children, we didn't have much money in our family. My father worked very hard and put many hours in, but with a family that big, there isn't much left for non-essentials. I knew if I wanted to have something my parents couldn't afford, I needed to find a way to earn extra money. This would have to be work above and beyond the daily chores my father would leave written in crayon on a paper grocery bag that each of us siblings were supposed to do. And keep in mind we didn't get an allowance. I would cut lawns in the neighborhood or shovel driveways in the winter for a few dollars. I even delivered the Detroit News as a paperboy which gave me a little income at the end of each month.

I quickly learned if I saved a good portion of the money each month in a savings account at the local bank, and didn't spend it all impulsively, I could have enough to pay for something I really needed, or have money over time for college. I knew the sacrifice I was making in the moment, but I also had a great sense of satisfaction in looking at the modest amount of increase each month in my savings account. If I had spent it all in some haphazard way, it would be as if the sacrifices I made never had happened.

When we look at the heroes we idolize in history and celebrate their legacy, we honor them by not only knowing their successes, but also their numerous setbacks. And in many ways their setbacks made them who they became, building the momentum for any movement that brought needed change to our world. The way to honor the legacy of our heroes is not only to continue their struggle today but to also move on through our own obstacles and keep pushing as they did in their time. We need to maintain.

The movement toward equal rights for people of color is a poignant tale for all of us in this regard. The path to justice was filled with moments of injustice. In a previous chapter, I mentioned the murder of Emmett Till, and the response of his family, the faith community and civil rights leaders to that miscarriage of justice. But there were so many more moments similar to this in the path to the promise land, and the response to each in the path to civil rights is instructive.

The civil rights advocates didn't just bury Till or Jimmy Lee Jackson or Medgar Evers, or James Chaney, Andrew Goodman or Michael Schwerner and so many more, erect a memorial, and move on with their lives. They honored these folks by continuing the movement and using their sacrifice as a way to empower the movement to call for justice. They knew that the best way to highlight the legacy of those who lost their lives was to get up from being knocked down or jailed, live out the legacy in their words and actions, and lead us all to a more just world.

In our moments of contemplation and introspection, we can each ask ourselves how we can ensure that the leaders we hoist up on a pedestal can more readily walk among us. How do we make sure they aren't forgotten and merely relegated to a history book or an exhibit in a museum? How are we practicing their ideals and living out their legacy today? How are we maintaining the landscape so it doesn't overgrow again, allowing the beautiful spirits of our heroes to disappear across our land?

There are generations arising as we speak who will feel called to some purpose or meaning in their life. You might even be one of those who is just graduating from high school or college, and about to set off on your own path in the world. I am sure you have come across personal heroes you've considered and felt kinship with as you have studied, opening your mind in your journey of learning and growing.

I ask you not only to consider the legacy you desire to honor, and to hold up figures from the present or past whom you admire, but also to consider what you might do to build your own legacy in this life. What are those values that you want to share, and what meaning do you want to instill in the circles of your world? Yes, you may want to do huge important things. You may want to run for office or start a company or become a judge or create great artistic work.

Those are all wonderful and beautiful motivating goals, but along the way, don't forget the meaning and impact on your legacy of some of the smallest and simplest things you can do in your life. Those seemingly small leadership moments can have profound consequences in the world around you. They can touch someone in ways that you can't predict. You may not be able to imagine how something you did or said will land and have a lasting impact in a mere moment.

In our remembering of others and in the revealing of our own legacies, we might ask ourselves, in the currents of regular living, how are we showing love, how are we revealing courage, how are we creating beauty, how are we walking in faith, how are we are pushing for justice, and how might we be creating hope in someone else's life.

Something I will never forget that has touched my heart to this day happened years ago when I was snowmobiling in Colorado. I was out on the narrow trails on a mountain side riding too fast and taking corners too sharp, and I ended up slamming at a high speed into a tree. I was taken down the mountain by some friends who knew I was seriously hurt.

I could hardly walk or breath. When I was checked out at the clinic in a pass of cleared trees in the mountains filled with snow, the doctors quickly called a helicopter to fly me to a hospital in Denver. When I was lifted onto the helicopter on a gurney, I was alone, far from home, and really nervous about my condition. The EMS person on board was a kind and caring woman who merely touched the side of my face and looked in my eyes and said, "It's going to be okay." I still can't recall her name, but I will never forget that kindness. She gave me hope in a moment when I was helpless and terrified. And I try to live out her touch as best I can with others.

This idea of creating and living out a legacy isn't just for the new generation of folks arising in our midst to consider. No matter your age, it is never too late to think of the imprint you want to leave on the world. It should not be of concern to us if we are retired, or just plain tired of the travails of life. We each have an opportunity to start anew, and to give meaning to our lives by honoring the legacy of those who have come before and putting thought into our own.

Grandma Moses, the great American folk artist, had always had a dream of painting and creating beauty in this world. Because of the circumstances of her life, the business of the daily routine and her attention to the needs of others, she set this dream aside and moved on. At the age of 78, she finally took up painting again in earnest. And for the remainder of her life, she gave the world a legacy of creativity and beauty.

Charles Darwin, the brilliant English scientist, took his famous Journey of the Beagle at age 21. But because of nervousness, anxiety and insecurity, he didn't publish his seminal work, *The Origin of the Species*, until he was 50. He finally realized later in life he needed to overcome his own internal roadblocks, and because he pushed past his fears, his legacy was established and is with us today.

Can we push through our own roadblocks and discover how best to give meaning to the legacy we applaud in others or to add to that legacy in making creative steps of our own no matter our station, position or time in our life? Can we discover what simple touch we can give another in a moment today that will move them even if they never remember our names? Can we bring to life the passages and words we have underlined in books we hold dear?

Legacies are especially difficult affairs for people who are born into prominent families who have had relatives come before them who achieved great things. The pressure they feel to just meet the expectations of the family history is immense, and for some can be completely overwhelming. This can be the case for someone born into a family of incredible wealth, fame or political office; the burden of their own family's legacy can be something hard to step out from, and there is often a lot of judgment and pressure from others to carry forward the family's legacy in the same way.

Think for a moment, though they were born into privilege, of the pressure that was put on future generations of Roosevelts, Kennedys, Kings and Gettys, and will be put on the future generations of Bushes, Obamas, Gates and Beyonces/Jay-Zs. Each of these new generations of "legacy children" will have to push out from under the shadows of their parents and grandparents and try to forge and ultimately live out their own legacies ahead.

Some advice from Mother Teresa who created a legacy of her own in service to others might be helpful to any one of us who is trying to cut a path and live a legacy in this moment and not be burdened by the past. When asked by others how they could follow her lead in what she was doing in India, she said, "Stay where you are. Find your own Calcutta. Find the sick, the suffering, and the lonely, right where you are—in your own homes and in your own families, in homes and in your workplaces and in your schools. You can find Calcutta all over the world, if you have eyes to see. Everywhere, wherever you go, you find people who are unwanted, unloved, uncared for, just rejected by society—completely forgotten, completely left alone."

As we endeavor to honor the legacy of someone, whether it be Mother Teresa, Martin Luther King, Jr. or even our own family circles—so that they won't be forgotten—and strive to build our own legacies so we won't have lived for naught, can we, as Bradbury suggested, "change something from the way it was before you touched it into something that's like you after you take your hands away."

Arch Rock

An opening to see beauty
Of a Lake speckled in colors
With sand softly caressing the shore
A bridge naturally
Through thousands of years
Of constant change and movement
On an island of no cars
Found by a walk
Through trails in the pines

Created through ages
Honored over time
By natives and travelers
Building bridges and beauty
Take a long time
A wave, a raindrop, a rock slide
Step by step
Touch by touch
The hardest stone will wilt
Under the caresses of the Earth
Leaving a legacy
Unforgotten and sought

10
Interconnections

"What's fun is that when you're no longer attached to being one separate part of it, you get to be part of all of it. At that point the 'all' is known to you sub-jectively, and you are everywhere at once, because you are no longer pinned in a space-time locus by your separateness. Metaphysics tell me that, and physics tell me that. Everything I have experienced in all my inner work points to that."

These words of Ram Dass—a spiritual teacher who was born Richard Alpert in 1931 in Boston, Massachusetts, and studied under a Hindu sacred man and guru Neem Karoli Baba, who gave him this new name—speak to a revelation that many of us never have until decades into our lives. It was very in late in my own life that I finally had some understanding of this reality of interconnections in a most simple unexpected moment.

For most of my life I thought the best position to be in was complete reliance on myself, and that solitude was the path to real peace, calm and purpose. Yes, I would have rela-tionships with others, but in the end, I relied on my own individuality. While creating connections to a larger world, I didn't trust in that connectivity more than as a temporary arrangement or fiction to get us through a complicated and difficult existence.

I was a bit of a follower of the attitude of the great filmmaker Orson Welles who said, "We're born alone, we live alone, we die alone. Only through our love and friendship can we create the illusion for the moment that we're not alone." While at an intellectual level I knew the importance and reality of connections, I didn't accept it deep down. I didn't *really* understand it. That all changed in an instant of epiphany for me, one that has been integrated in my life through a series of lessons since.

After a long run on a quiet country road here in Texas, in the midst of wilting summer heat on one of those typical one-hundred-degree days, I went inside, parched and drenched in sweat. I was getting a cold drink of water at my sink in the house and staring out the window across the land. The sun was shining bright, the deer were slowly walking across the Texas limestone near the Live Oak trees, the black turkey vultures were circling in the sky, and the swallows on my porch were resting in their nest in the shade under the roof.

And I suddenly had this most profound sense of how everything in this universe was so beautifully interconnected. It was a complete understanding and vision of how everything I was looking at out the window was all universally connected, along with myself and every other being I could not see. The intense feeling passed after a few moments, but the thought embedded its way into me, like a dream you wake up from that you think is real and stays with you for days, popping back into your mind and heart over and over.

When one thinks about the beginnings of the universe that scientists believe all sprung from one "big bang" more than 14 billion years ago, we realize everything that exists started out from one singularity in a sole dense bit of space. And from this singularity, matter expanded outward and continues to expand in unknown areas of the universe. Thus we all began as and belong to the same original matter.

It is fascinating that both scientific treatises as well as many of our sacred texts have come to the same conclusion about this interconnection. The acclaimed astrophysicist Carl Sagan wrote, "The cosmos is within us. We are made of star-stuff. We are a way for the universe to know itself." And in the Old Testament in Ecclesiastes it is written, "All go to one place. All are from the dust, and to dust all return," and these are roughly the same words those of us in the Christian faith repeat on each Ash Wednesday as we enter the religious time of Lent. We are all composed in some way of the same building block material of the universe, and we are connected in fundamental ways.

Before one begins to settle into this truth and examine what it might mean in our daily interactions and judgments, let us also look at how interconnected the expanse of history might be. When one considers the movements of time, politics, culture and human endeavors, we realize how often change doesn't occur in just one area of life. When disruptions or unrelenting change—and then subsequent adjustments and resolutions to this change—evolve in one aspect of the world, these changes almost always reveal themselves in many other areas simultaneously. As movement occurs in one area, it is happening in many other areas concurrently.

In a column I wrote a few years ago, I focused on two mystics of different faiths whose time on this planet overlapped nearly one thousand years ago. And these two faith traditions at the time were in violent conflict with each other, the kind of conflict we still seem to be experiencing in ways today. Though these two wise men certainly never met, they were connected in the unfolding of the universe and in ways we are likely to never fully comprehend.

The Muslim poet Rumi was born in Persia in 1207, and his writings provided the people who read his work a new perspective of the world and life. A few thousand miles away, an Italian Catholic friar from Assisi named Francis lived, and by his simple, yet profound, acts of compassion and caring changed his community and an entire church. Both Rumi and Francis still influence us today.

Both of these men came of age in a time of great change and upheaval, a time of bloody conflict between followers of Islam and Christianity. Both Rumi and St. Francis, through their words and actions, preached a path of love, forgiveness and understanding. While each was informed by different faiths, families and local environments, their messages couldn't have been more similar and soulful.

These thoughtful and heart-driven men believed that we are all part of the same universe created by God, interconnected in more ways than we will ever know, and that our most important obligation is to care for each other as we would ourselves, and follow a path of universal love. Love drove the words they communicated, whether in poems or preaching, and the actions they took in their communities to lift up their fellow human beings.

Each concentrated on the values, dreams and desires we all share as human beings, and not on the differences between us, whether it be language, ritual, manners or even faiths. Francis reached out with a humble and open hand and heart to those of Muslim faith, even while bloodshed between Christians and Muslims surrounded him. He wanted to follow the path of love Jesus Christ laid down a thousand years before him. A path the Catholic Church had diverged drastically from in his time.

Francis realized that the truest path to God was recognizing the divinity that exists within each of us, whether we are rich or poor, healthy or sick, revered or unknown. And that upon that divine recognition, our purpose becomes one of compassion and love reflected in the manner we care for each other.

Rumi wrote thousands of amazing poems and words, in a language and alphabet Francis couldn't read, about the beauty of love and the power it has to change one's own heart and those surrounding us. Rumi also lived in an environment where hate toward Christians and others not of his faith burned like a bonfire all around him. And he, like St. Francis, believed that hate would only destroy the good in us, and the true path of faith was built with bricks of love and mortar of truth and understanding. Ever the devout and faithful Muslim, Rumi is quoted as saying, "Christian, Jew, Muslim, shaman, Zoroastrian, stone, ground, mountain, river, each has a secret way of being with the mystery, unique and not to be judged."

Closer to home here in America, we see similarly how when disruptions and change occur in our nation, they happen in multiple areas simultaneously. At each moment, though, we tend to compartmentalize aspects of American life, not always recognizing that there is integrated change happening across the expanse. Our own national history points to the interconnections of time and space.

For example, as the United States was in the midst of conflict running up to and during the Civil War, with regions and values in volatile opposition, the United States was undergoing immense economic change with the advent of the Industrial Revolution and migration from farms into cities for work. Further, our communications were advancing quickly with the widespread use of the electrical telegraph system spread from ocean to ocean. Waves of new immigrants had come to America, including my Irish ancestors, bringing deep and lasting cultural change.

In the 1930s we again had economic disruptions with the Great Depression. This was coupled with new waves of immigrants and further geographic movements as families continued to uproot themselves and flock into urban settings leaving their small towns and rural life. And the world was in disintegration, as nearly every country was dragged ultimately into the midst of the global conflict, World War II. Communications were also advancing quickly with widespread use of radio, and the beginning stages of television. All of these came at once in varied areas affecting every American's life.

We are in the midst of an awakening to our own broad interconnectedness today. A virus affecting us all has spread to every nook and cranny of our country, leaving no one unaffected. The face of American life continues to change in dramatic fashion with new immigrant arrivals and increasing diversity at every level. Important debates and discussions are unfolding about how we might change our constitutional structures as an emerging multiethnic democracy. There are incredible cultural conflicts surrounding institutions and symbols that were the norm of American life for years. A changing economy; global climate change; and advances in communications because of the internet, satellites and universal use of cell phones are all evolutions affecting us today.

We, too often, look at our present, and complain no one has ever faced these interconnected changes before. One only has to do a cursory review of our country's history to see how the past proves that complaint lacks proper perspective. The universe has consistently sent us messages, in varied ways, over time reminding us of how we are all bound together in so many different ways.

Recently, I went to visit Montgomery, Alabama, to walk the path through some of the key parts of the civil rights movement. I, once again, came away with that revelation of how interconnected life is and how close we all are in so many ways. Too often we only focus on the differences and divisions, and we don't sit with how united we are through the changes in fundamental values like love of family, fairness and justice, and hope for our future, and how so many seemingly disparate parts line up in astounding ways.

Standing on the Alabama State Capitol steps in Montgomery beneath a sunny winter sky, I realized that this is where, over different times, the head of the Confederacy Jefferson Davis took his oath of office, where Dr. Martin Luther King, Jr. gave a key speech in the March for Freedom, and where civil rights icon John Lewis' casket recently lay after a procession from Selma to Montgomery commemorating that march where King spoke years earlier. In that moment I imagined if I was a baseball player (baseball being the American pastime and a sport I have always loved) standing on the steps and the area in front of me was a baseball stadium...what would happen if I hit a few balls?

A single down third base would end up in the yard of the Confederate White House, a double could land in the church yard where King was a pastor, two long centerfield home runs would make it to both the spot Rosa Parks got on the fateful bus ride and to the fountain where slaves were once sold, and a foul ball behind me could land on the roof of the Kings' home where a bomb was thrown on his steps.

I imagined stands surrounding this small area full of folks who tried to prevent justice and equality for people of color and those pushing for civil rights and an equal place in society—each cheering on their own side in this incredible conflict, which is unfortunately still with us today. Fans of opposite political sides with one side fighting for expanded democracy, diversity and equality, and another side cheering on restrictions on voting rights, curtailing immigration and fearing equality.

The interconnectedness of our world isn't just about broad societal change and effects, it is also about how change is connected in our own smaller worlds. The macro of the universe always has lessons for the micro of our lives, and the micro of our lives can also tell the tales of the macro of all existence. What change occurs in each and how we connect tells the story for both the world writ large and for each of us in our lives in our personal relationships and relatedness.

In my own life as I look back, I realize that as disruptions occurred, and as I examined the ways I desired to build meaning, those disruptions involved more than just one aspect and included each part of my humanity. Significant transformations in multiple aspects of my life worked together as a whole. More than a decade ago in one brief period, I went through a divorce, changed where I lived and simplified my possessions, and had a fundamental change in my professional life when I had a very public break with President Bush for whom I had served as chief strategist. All of these happened all at once.

I didn't set out to change everything at one time, I just knew in some heart or soul space that the meaning and purpose of my world needed to change. And as I took one step, one alteration in one area, it emerged that I needed to take other steps, other changes in other areas. As I designed one aspect of my life differently, I naturally felt drawn to change others so that my life, in a more complete way, was more aligned with my internal heart intention.

Yes, it was difficult and caused stress to do this all at once, but since who we are with, what we do, and where we spend our time are so interconnected, it felt more stressful to me not to segment my life into artificial boxes but to let things unfold and make decisions being aware of the interrelationship that the universe seems to constantly remind us of.

When we examine all the changes that have come our way recently and the incredible disruptions of each of our lives, we too often focus on what happens to us, and not enough on what we can actively change in order for ripples to occur in a more positive way in our world and the world at large. Just as negative changes seem to be connected and happen all at once, so too positive change and solutions must occur in the same way.

Because of the interrelatedness of life and the interconnections of the universe, how we solve problems and difficulties also must be approached in a similar manner of integration. We can't, and couldn't, conquer the coronavirus unless we each changed various aspects of our behavior, including what we wear, how we act, how we gather, and how we voted for leaders who know what they are doing and who could take their own part in solving the problem. We can't solve the inequities of our economy unless we all participate in the solution depending upon our platform or purpose. Climate change and its effects can't be dealt with unless we each participate in the solution at every level, including the choices we make each day in how we live. The integration of all solutions is the only possible way to fix and address the larger issues of our society.

And thusly the interconnectedness of our individual lives must also be addressed in an interrelated way. In order to find meaning and purpose that leads to joy and peace for ourselves, we need to step forward and make decisions that acknowledge we are interconnected in ways we both understand clearly and in ways that are still a mystery.

I quoted earlier an excerpt from Dr. Martin Luther King's letter from a Birmingham jail, and his words speak a fundamental truth in this regard for not only his time in the 1960s, but also for today. He wrote, "In a real sense all life is inter-related. All men are caught in an inescapable network of mutuality, tied in a single garment of destiny. Whatever affects one directly, affects all indirectly. I can never be what I ought to be until you are what you ought to be, and you can never be what you ought to be until I am what I ought to be...This is the inter-related structure of reality."

Each of us knows that how our neighbor is and what they do, while seemingly separate from us, can either consciously or unconsciously affect us. And what we do or say has the same effect on our neighbors. As I stood on the banks of the Blanco River fishing in a deep spot, I thought about how what somebody might dump or pollute way upstream would affect me and the fish right here. And so too what I might dump in the river on my property will certainly affect many people downstream. And so, it is if I clean up something in the river on my land, it will help others farther away that I may never know.

Our lives and our deaths, because of the nature of interconnections, give us such incredible power to move the world in positive ways. The small steps we can take, because of the interrelatedness of mankind and nature, give us incredible power. But if we only look at the world in a segmented fashion, we don't see that, and we may think what we do doesn't matter. Even when we pass from this Earth, we can continue to give in the circle of life in what we leave behind. The lives we have touched and nourished, whether it be children, friends or strangers, will pay it forward even as we go back to our origin of dust.

An Integrated Life

A deer fallen
Swept down the river
Wedged in a crevice
A life lived
In nature fulfilled
Turkey vultures arrive
Gather in the Cypress
Then fly above
Sensing below
Discovering a meal
The deer gives once more
An integrated life
We can each keep giving

Long after we think
Bones picked clean
Left white and pecked
On the river bottom
New deer come
And walk the banks
Remember the life
Of a fallen friend
Vultures fly off
Having done their duty
Cleaning the Earth
Each a part
Of each other

Conclusion

"When you reach the end of what you should know, you will be at the beginning of what you should sense."

These words of poet and philosopher Kahlil Gibran cross the span of time and distance from a poet philosopher who was born in 1863 in Lebanon and became known by the world from his seminal work, *The Prophet.* And the truth of what he reveals speaks to us in this moment of our lives. As we recover from the last few years of turbulence, turmoil and tensions, and chart our course ahead, let us pay heed to Gibran in understanding that we must move beyond what we know with our heads, and begin again where our hearts can inspire us.

I first became acquainted with Gibran in college in St. Louis as I began to step out in the world in my own way, and to discover meaning and find what truth most resonated with and inspired me. You might be beginning that same journey as you move away from home out of high school into college, where you begin now being finally considered an adult in many ways. Or you could possibly be on the verge of leaving college, to go out into the world with purpose to begin some profession or further study. Or you could be like me and so many others, who later in life are taking steps into a second act. Figure out where you find discomfort and lean into it, sense where you are frustrated and explore why, and begin to do things with some amount of introspection. You, like all of us, had a year you did not expect, one that likely confused and frustrated you, but know that it proved your grit, resilience and ability to adapt.

As I left high school, I knew I wanted to become involved in politics. When I entered college as I studied political science and volunteered on campaigns, I also realized that to be in politics, public speaking was a necessity. Ever since I was young, I always had a fear of public speaking. You couldn't pay me (and no one would at that time) to speak in front of a group of people. I knew I had to expose myself to talking with groups of folks if I wanted to be successful in my chosen profession. So I decided to volunteer for as many moments of public speaking as I could while in college in order to raise questions in myself, to see what might be revealed, and to build up new muscles. I ended up agreeing to more than 100 speaking engagements, and it didn't matter the audience size.

Often, we assume as we look out at other successful leaders that those people are somehow born into what they do and are naturally gifted in what we know them for in their professions. People assume that since I ended up in high-profile positions in politics where public speaking was a daily occurrence, and appear on television for various news platforms, that I do it all naturally. This certainly wasn't true for me, and I've learned that's the case for so many others I have encountered in the world.

I remember when I first met television host and comedian Stephen Colbert before I was going to appear on *The Colbert*

Show. I was struck in the meeting in his eclectic office how intro-
verted and unassuming he came across. He, like me, grew up
in a family of 11 children, and waded through lots of fear and
trauma like each one of us. Colbert dealt with tragic hardship
some of us may find difficult to imagine: in 1974, when Colbert was 10 years old, his father and his two brothers nearest in
age, Peter and Paul, were killed in the crash of an Eastern Air-
lines flight while it was attempting to land in Charlotte, North
Carolina. Stephen is a Catholic, like myself, and a person of
devoted faith; he's an avid reader, constantly pushing himself,
and exploring the uncomfortable to see what might be revealed
about himself and others.

As you have read through these topics of love, trauma, past/
present/future, ends/means, faith/science, light and dark, forgiveness, concentric circles, legacy, and interconnection, I hope
it moves you to your own insights into revelations that you might
have had in the past and didn't pay attention to. Or maybe it
will spur some greater attention to epiphanies that might come
to you in the days and years ahead. As we each move forward
in this time of disruption, disconnection and disappointment,
let us understand how these concepts can guide us in finding
and creating meaning and direction. I hope that you will find
inspiration and continue to dream even in the aftermath of
challenging times—dreams that over the last few years might
have been deferred, delayed or even dropped.

The most pointed revelations that have occurred in my life
were realized while going through some difficult or tragic time,
in the aftermath of reading a moving passage, or in the midst
of a profound, joyful or sorrowful experience. Each of these
moments raised questions or mysteries so that I then began to

search for answers. It is in the search that we discover who we are, how we might change direction, what it is that inspires us and what we most desire in life. And I am still trying to push myself into uncomfortable places in order for more questions to arise, and in those places reading becomes a safe harbor for me, which I hope this has been for you.

As we think of love, what it all means, and how we relate to others, maybe you are in a unique circumstance. Maybe you just fell in love, or just fell out of love. Maybe you are questioning your relationship with the Almighty, or have a renewed sense of faith that you are trying to define, or maybe you don't believe in God but sense a love of something bigger that goes beyond self. Maybe you are trying to figure out the dynamic you want with family and friends, or maybe in this moment, you would love a time of solitude.

Here are some additional questions that might help in exploration as you ponder: What is your earliest memory of feeling loved? What is it about others or the world that you hate, and what does this reveal about what it is you love? What frustrates you about your nation or neighborhood, and how does that uncover what you love? Do you wonder if you will ever experience a deep loving bond, do you look for it out there in the universe? Have you taken the time to really look inward and see if any blocks to love you may have are within your own heart?

Trauma and fears often hold us back from being our best self. Some of these are real and terribly difficult, some we tie to our identity and carry with us thinking they are integral to who we are, and some are myths that we thought we needed to keep alive to protect ourselves. Many of our fears and traumas are individually experienced, while some affect our communities or country and become part of our collective experience.

Have you described your traumas or fears to another person you trust and opened up about it even though it scares you? Have you seriously contemplated when you make fundamental important choices whether you are being driven by fear or by love? Have you felt where it is in your body when you have been anxious or angry for no real apparent or direct reason? When you are in fear, have you taken a moment to pause and not rush to a decision? Do you know each of us carries trauma in some way and so you aren't alone?

Yes, you are alive in this present here and now, reading these words, and hopefully at peace as you contemplate your place in the world and what moves you in your life. I hope you also know that your past is what brought you to this present, and it is what made you who you are, in all your dark and light, securities and insecurities. Don't forget that past and how you overcame as you create a vision for your future. All of it is a gift. As you stay present, I hope you simultaneously understand and take responsibility for your past, and can look forward to a future that you can define even if it is a broad vision.

Do you at times try to deny something in your past because it weighs too much on your present or you worry it will infect your future? Can you step back and bring resolution to something in your past, perhaps through accepting your own accountability? Is there a way you can relax in that acceptance and see how the dots of your past connect to your present and will lead to your dreams ahead? Are you carrying feelings in your present that are associated with incidents from your past? Can you accept that time is really a fiction that we have created and that the past, present and future are all one?

As you create and construct your life and your path ahead and decisions you need to make, focus your time and efforts less on the ends and more on the means of the process and how you want to be in this world. The wisest people in history, from faith to politics, understood that it is the means of how we are and our values that define us, and not the ends. Yes, put a finishing line out there in the marathon of your life, but look more at how you are stepping into your world and how you are relating to others.

If you want to earn a living and need money, do you think it is okay to cut corners and not always behave with integrity? Do you want to get in better shape or become healthier but look for a short cut that speeds up the process, missing out on the daily satisfaction of making healthy decisions and implementing new habits? Do you want a particular political party or ideology in office and think it is okay to use nefarious means to get there? Can you have faith deep down in the idea that if the means are worthy, then the ends will be good?

Knowledge and wisdom are crucial as we each venture out into this world and make our way. Faith can go hand in hand with the search for knowledge and truth. Wisdom can come to us in so many varied forms. Yes, insights involve our minds, but epiphanies also come through our hearts and souls. We can simultaneously have faith in something bigger than ourselves, whether it is God or something else, and realize there are so many mysteries in the universe, while also understanding that science and mindful methods of inquiry uncover truth and reveal where myths of the past need to be discarded. Faith and science can partner together for us to lead this world to greater enlightenment and our own spiritual and mental evolution as beings.

If you believe in God, do you allow for the truth that God creates our doubts and our striving for knowledge? If you don't believe in God, do you accept that some belief in something greater than yourself allows us to sacrifice when needed for the greater good, understanding the connection and divinity among us all? Can you pick political leaders who understand the integration of faith and science and accept others' paths without judgment? Can you be humble in the understanding that you may have unique knowledge, but so do others? Can you learn from the wisdom of past generations while also honoring your own revelations and individual path?

Each of us holds spaces of light and dark in our hearts and souls. It is that light and dark that allow for the shades of this world, and the dance of shadows that beautifully make us who we are as flawed and amazing human beings. In those darkest times in our life, we understand the beauty when light comes to us or when we bring light to others; it is the dark that reveals the light. As we search across the horizon, whether the waters are still or choppy, we realize that others are there as a lighthouse welcoming us to a safe harbor or warning us of danger. And if we don't see that lighthouse, maybe this is a call for us to be that on the shore.

As you celebrate your own positive aspects and light, have you also uncovered your darkness that you may have been hiding not only from others but yourself? When you are looking for a light, have you considered maybe the light you need is turning on something inside you to shine for another? Do you understand that even a country as wonderful as yours has a history of both light and dark that must be explored and acknowledged? Though lighthouses for me are a great symbol, do you have a better one for you that enhances your understanding of light and dark?

We each deeply want reconciliation in those spaces and places in our lives that have conflicts and disagreements. But let us not jump too quickly to striving for unity before we have some examination of the truth and we assess accountability for the problem or rift. When we jump too quickly to bring everyone together as one big happy family, this prolongs the problem because it just buries the issue momentarily. First, we need to step back and assess accountability (our own and others'), and all parties need to consider forgiveness. And the path to forgiveness is a process that has multiple steps, but in the end, it is forgiveness of another that frees us from our own blockages.

Have you accepted your own accountability in some problem and admitted the truth of your own responsibility? Have you given someone else the time to process through their mistakes and not hurriedly tried to get an apology? Have you said "I am sorry" too readily so that another questions the authenticity of your desire for true forgiveness? Do you want to resolve the conflict quickly and superficially rather than processing any pain it may be causing? Can you apply what you know about our personal processes of reconciliation to your country as well?

In the organization of our own individual world, and how we relate to each other, we can consider the series of concentric circles in our lives. This can allow for a better understanding of the ebb and flow of communicating with one another. We don't have to trust or love everyone the same, and we aren't required to welcome even the people we are close to into every intimate area of our life. We can compassionately set boundaries that not only protect us but protect our friends and family by not trusting where we shouldn't, or not distrusting where we should trust. And we must always remember no matter how far out someone is in our circles, we must still be receptive to communication from others so we can adapt and more effectively earn trust.

Can you take a moment and really figure out where people belong in the concentric circles of your life? Who or what is in your innermost circle, and have you told them of this so they are aware and can be responsible? Are there people you have welcomed in your innermost circle who it might be necessary to move out to a different place? Are you open to receiving input from all the circles of your life in appropriate ways so you can keep learning and change if you need to?

Each of us has heroes in life, and we have clear reasons why those folks are heroes, largely because of the legacies they've left behind. And these heroes are not just someone famous or figures in a history book, they are also are our mothers or fathers, our children, local leaders in our communities, or people whose names we may not even be able to remember. And the most meaningful way we can honor the legacy of these heroes is not by a plaque or statue, but by living our life aligned with the values that signified their life. We can also recall the ideals and legacy that were the basis for our country's founding and push for our values today to be in alignment with things like justice, equality and authentic leadership in the spirit of service to others.

Who are your heroes and what fundamental values do they represent? Where in your own life today are those values present, and where might you create clear opportunities for alignment? Do you need to reorganize or simplify your world so you can better live out that legacy? Are you a hero in some way for another or a group, and are you cognizant of your responsibility in what you say or do? What leaders are you aware of that others might not be who would be good legacy models, and how you can support them?

As I write this on Ash Wednesday in the midst of a terrible winter storm in Texas where millions are without power and water, I again am clearly aware of how interconnected we all are. It doesn't matter who you are or where you live, the decisions we make and those that others make have a ripple effect across millions of human beings. We each are a part of another, and the natural world is part of all of us in both its beauty and in its destructiveness. We are all born from the same stuff, and there is an interrelationship amongst every single thing, both animate and inanimate. And we each bear a tremendous responsibility in what we say and do or what we allow in this world, whether we see the extent of the effect or not.

What decision did you make today that affected another? What did you read about in the news of something happening far away that you felt had a profound effect on you? Does it empower you when you understand how interconnected we all are, or does it overwhelm you? Where is it in nature for you uniquely that you feel, in the depth of your soul, connected to all that is around you? What small steps can you make in words or deeds that might highlight in a positive way the interrelationship of each of us?

Our time has come to a close, and I wish you all the strength, courage and wisdom you might need in designing your life around these fundamentals and possibly continuing to redesign your life no matter what stage you're in during your time here on Earth. I hope you know how much you matter to this world, and the incredible impact you can have with your unique talents and attributes. Some days you will need to rest and recuperate, and other days you will have the energy, stamina and inspiration to make great leaps. I am confident you can do it. The world is waiting for you. And I will cheer you on from down on the Blanco River.

A Way Appears

The hill rises
Above the expanse
Rolling down to the river
Venturing out confidently
The entrance is clear
Hiking for a time
On an easy path
Cleared by others
Then, it stops
Broken trees, rocks, thorny bushes
Covering the way forward
Which direction to go
Which way is best
I pause, I quiet
Letting the breeze
Sweep gently
On my skin
Closing my eyes

Whispering to me
A hymn, a memory
"Let the way appear"
It is then revealed
An old deer trail
Fresh to me
Winding around
Following that route
I reach the summit
Sometimes stillness
Gives one fresh direction
And we discover
A new way home

About the Author

Matthew Dowd, a renowned thought-leader and writer, is one of the most creative analysts, visionaries, and political strategists of his generation, serving as a key advisor on over one hundred political campaigns—for both major political parties and at every level of government—and a trusted influential voice, author, and media analyst known for bringing a common-sense perspective to cultural, political, economic, and spiritual trends.

Dowd was born in Detroit, Michigan, the third of eleven children in an Irish-Catholic family. His first job was as a paperboy delivering the *Detroit News*, and then as a caddy at a suburban Detroit country club, learning early lessons about people, values, and life that still stay an integral part of him. From a very young age, his love of reading took him on a path of faith and spirituality, themes that have remained a strong focus throughout his life. When he was only twelve years old, the Watergate hearings captivated him along with the nation, instilling in him a love of politics, the importance of leadership based on integrity, and a belief in public service.

Dowd began his career as an aide for Congressman Richard Gephardt (D-Missouri) in St. Louis, MO, which led to opportunities to work for Congressman J. J. "Jake" Pickle (D-Texas), the Texas Democratic Party, and as field director for Congressman Jim Chapman's 1985 special election win in East Texas. His ascension in national politics began with the vice-presidential campaign of US Senator Lloyd Bentsen in 1988, after which he served throughout the 1990s as chief strategist for Texas Lieutenant Governor Bob Bullock, the last high-profile Democrat to win statewide in Texas. After being named a rising national star by *Campaigns & Elections* magazine, in recognition of his work around the country, and leaving a public relations company he co-founded, Public Strategies, Inc, he was tapped to serve as director of media and polling in the successful presidential campaign for Texas Governor George W. Bush in 2000. He served as chief strategist and is widely credited for employing groundbreaking techniques for Bush's successful re-election campaign in 2004, after which he was named strategist of the year by a bipartisan association of political consultants. He later served as chief strategist for California Governor Arnold Schwarzenegger's successful gubernatorial 2006 re-election campaign.

In 2007 Dowd publicly broke with President Bush and the Republican Party, declaring himself an independent; he left political campaigns and co-authored the *New York Times* bestseller *Applebee's America: How Successful Political, Business, and Religious Leaders Connect with the New American Community* (2006). He then joined with colleagues to form Vianovo, Inc., a media and public relations firm that advised numerous foundations, campaigns, and corporations—including the Bill and Melinda Gates Foundation, the National Basketball Association, and Bono's ONE Campaign. He later founded CountryOverParty, a national forum to convene voters and candidates dedicated to a leadership vision that prioritized values such as integrity, compassion, honesty, decency, service, and dedication to patriotism over party affiliation.

From 2008 until January 2021, Dowd was the chief political analyst for ABC News, becoming a reliable, steady voice for over a decade for fact-based, non-partisan insights on *Good Morning America*, *This Week*, and *Nightline*. During that time, he published the groundbreaking bestseller *A New Way: Embracing the Paradox as We Lead and Serve* (2017), along with hundreds of columns on topics stretching from faith, spirituality, politics, and the dynamics and meaning of life for a variety of outlets including the *Washington Post*, *National Journal*, *USA Today*, the *New York Times*, and ABC News. He also served as a visiting lecturer at dozens of the nation's top universities, including Harvard, Yale, Stanford, Dartmouth, the University of Texas, the University of Chicago, and the USC Annenberg School for Communication and Journalism.

As a philanthropist, Dowd has invested in a number of startups around the county and has served on the boards of the Catholic non-profit Seton Family of Hospitals, Texas Habitat for Humanity, and Texas Impact, an interfaith group of people of all faiths working on behalf of justice. He is a proud "pop" of six wonderful children, four of whom who have grown into beautiful adults and two who he lost at a young age but will never forget. He lives a serene life amongst the beauty of nature on the Blanco River in Wimberley, Texas.